"Read this book to transform your job and life. Your boss will thank you and reward you for becoming the rarest of all things – an wonderfully engaged team member. What a difference it would have made when I worked for my entrepreneur!"

Ross Slater, President, Metris Group Inc.

"Wow! An incredibly insightful and practical book for every team member who's dreamt of having a better career. Chock full of practical tools, and written in a easy-to-read conversational style, you learn HOW to think about your job, not just about how to do it better. I highly recommend it."

Shannon Waller, Coach and Team Program Designer,
The Strategic Coach, Inc.
Co-author, *Unique Ability: Creating the Life You Want*

"Insightful, original, and chock full of spot-on advice for anyone who wants to exceed in working for an entrepreneur. And, if you are an entrepreneur and are aching for a team that will work with you to build your business to greatness, this book should be required reading for everyone in your company."

Teresa Byrd Morgan, Principal,
Morgan Law Center for Estate & Legacy Planning, PLLC
and Chairperson, The Florida Bar/Solo Small Firm Section

"This is a unique and powerful guide unlike any out there, authored by two remarkable women who have actually been there, just like you. Don't Be a Yes Chick! is filled with practical steps you can take starting right now to STOP feeling frustrated, held down, overwhelmed, and like you're just a pawn in someone else's game, and instead START experiencing the career respect, advancement, and deep satisfaction that should be yours. If you truly want to love your job -- and your life -- do yourself a favor and read this remarkable book!"

Brian Vaszily, world-renowned business and life coach,
founder of IntenseExperiences.com, one of the world's most popular
personal transformation destinations, and author of
The 9 Intense Experiences: An Action Plan to Change Your Life Forever

"A sassy, butt-kicking, wake-up call to the career you've always dreamed of."

Andrea Costantine, co-author of *Speaking Your Truth*

Don't Be a
YES CHICK!

*How to stop babysitting your boss, transform
your job, and work with a dream team without
losing your sanity or your spirit in the process*

Molly Hall and Laney Lyons

Don't Be a Yes Chick!

Copyright © 2011 Molly Hall & Laney Lyons

www.yeschick.com

ISBN 978-0-615-47895-1

First Edition

10 9 8 7 6 5 4 3 2

DEDICATION

For my consistent rocks; Dad, Mom, Shaun, Aidan and Ella. Without each of your never-ending faith and allowance of time and space, this book would not be possible. – Molly Hall

For my mom - thank you for teaching me the value of kindness and the power of quiet courage. For Anwar - thank you for showing me that love can be selfless and joyful. – Laney Lyons

Table of Contents

Preface

"Champions aren't made in the ring,
they are merely recognized there. What you cheat on
in the early light of morning will show up
in the ring under the bright lights."

- Joe Frazier

Are you stuck in a rut in your career? Do you feel somewhere deep inside that your work should be more fulfilling–that this can't be all that you were meant to do?

Sometimes you may love what you do, but you may feel out of control due to your work environment. You might be frustrated by your company's general "climate," which may include chaos and lack of efficiency that may cause you to leave work feeling overwhelmed because you couldn't complete everything you needed to do.

Perhaps you are in a new job and are hoping that this will be "the one." If so, you may be nervous or tentative about showing your talents, skill sets, and full potential to your new boss.

Maybe you love your work and your co-workers, but you feel ready to take on more responsibility to advance in your career.

Are you unsure where to get what you need to fulfill your future? Are you considering going back to school, getting more training or certifications, or searching for a new, more fulfilling job?

Whether you are feeling out of control or uninspired in your current job or excited about a new one, *Don't Be a Yes Chick!* is for you. It's a no-degree-required, no-night-classes-needed way to take control of your professional life and *learn to run your office, and stop letting it run you.* This book will help you realize your personal passion and position it in your professional life. That's right; we just said "passion" and "professional" in the same sentence! It *is* possible–just like it's possible to achieve success at work while keeping boundaries between your work and personal time.

In *Yes Chick!* we will break through many sugarcoated clichés like, "Leave your personal life at the door" and "The boss is always right." Let's be real. Sometimes, you just *can't* leave it at the door, and the boss *isn't* always right! But how do you deal with that workplace mentality? Here we'll teach you not only how to deal with it, but how to turn it to your advantage and allow you to excel.

This book was written for you, by people *just like you*. We walk the walk and talk the talk of a time-stressed, overachieving, and worked-our-way-up professional, just like you. Of course, we go by many names. We have been known as "assistant," "secretary," "administrative assistant" "support staff," "my right hand," and even a far-flung anachronism such as "Girl Friday." *Ouch!* We're sure that at some point in your career, you have been or will be referred to as, "My assistant, who really does all the work" (usually uttered by your boss, with tongue firmly planted in cheek and a poke in the ribs to one of his or her colleagues). Oh, but didn't you realize this was meant to be a compliment? Have you ever wondered why it doesn't feel like one?

You could go to work wearing a tiara, sit on a throne, and change your title to the Queen of (insert company name here), but that wouldn't change a thing. And none of these "titles" defines who you are or what you do.

"What do you do?" When people ask that question in a social setting, how do you answer it anyway? "Princess?" Or do you tell them the truth–that you juggle *your own tasks* while reminding your boss of his or her own; you balance *your urgent needs* with your boss's; you grab the phones for the receptionist who is late, out sick, or taking a break; you prepare important documents for a presentation your boss needs in 20 minutes; and that you return five phone calls for said boss, who of course didn't have time? (And gleefully mention that you do all this during the lunch hour you never take.)

You will find this book radically different from others in the "professional growth" section of the bookstore. We are people just like you. We have no fancy degrees and no background in industrial or occupational psychology–just blood, sweat, tears, and tried-and-true methods that we learned and perfected in the ultimate field of battle–the almighty office!

Within these pages, you will not only learn how to survive life and work with a boss, you will also know how to *find your dreams* and *have the meaningful, fulfilling life you always wanted*. That doesn't mean you have to jump up and quit your job while wandering aimlessly around trying to "find yourself"! We've never understood why "finding yourself" has to mean being unemployed and without a plan. In this book, we'll teach you how to find your dreams without losing the progress you've already made in your career. You may even find them closer to home, or the office, than you think. If you don't, you will be armed with the tools to recognize them.

If you are reading this book, you are the type of person who "gets things done." You are probably the person people always call on when they have a problem—to solicit your opinions or to look to someone they can trust to get the job done. While that might be a great compliment, those intangible qualities are hard to express on a resume. You can't list them as a skill or certification. There is no degree in "Trust me to get it done." Often, and ironically, the inability to articulate and measure this quality results in you being *underpaid, under-promoted,* and *under-appreciated.* This book will teach you how to harness those "human-to-human" skills, develop them, and be able to clarify them to those for whom you work. It will result in *more money, more respect,* and *more personal satisfaction for you.*

Introduction

Y ou might be wondering who we are and what makes us qualified to write this book. We both work for entrepreneurs and help them run their businesses. We aren't highly paid CEOs with business degrees. We are the ones who get things done, the "right hands" who do everything from marketing and sales to making coffee, collaborating with power partners, and feverishly running billing when Friday payroll is looking like its about to throw everything in the red.

Note from Molly Hall

How many of you are sitting in the exact position I was, on the hamster wheel, making "good enough" money but with no idea where you will be 12 years from now? Let me save you 12 years and provide you with the direct access to creating a life you want by design and not by default.

If someone had told me 12 years ago that I would be sitting where I am today, I would never have believed it. Back then, I was living in my hometown of Buffalo, N.Y., working full-time for the city at The Neighborhood Revitalization Corporation, while at the same time working 40 hours a week in my family's Irish tavern in South Buffalo as a bartender, cook, and waitress. I was making a ton of money and having an absolute blast. I tried college but found it impossible to manage a class load while working two full-time jobs, so I entered "the real world" and quickly got used to having money. I lived this life for eight years until the day my dad decided he was ready to retire and handed his successful business over to my older sister and me.

My sister was ready to start a family, and I realized the "real world" *had* to be something better. I had never left my hometown in my entire life. In fact, I didn't even move out of my parents' house until I was 23. However, a close friend of mine was living in Denver, and we talked frequently. When my dad sold the bar, I was also able to take a one-year personal leave of absence from my city job. All signs seemed to point to "go," so I decided to leave my job, sell everything, and travel across-country for five weeks to give the Mile-High City a try.

Just three hours outside of Buffalo, I panicked and turned to my friend Judy, who was driving me across the country. "Judy, I can't do this. I'm going back to Buffalo." Judy turned to me without skipping a beat and said, "The way I see it, you have nothing to go back to, so treat this like a five-week vacation."

Three weeks after arriving in Denver, I began working for an attorney who specialized in estates and trusts, and I am still there today. When I took this first job, at the National Network of Estate Planning Attorneys, I had no idea that I was on the path to creating a lifetime profession. Over the past 12 years I have worked closely with presidents and founders of national organizations, master marketers, entrepreneurs, and coaches. I can't help but practice the "coach" way of doing things on a daily basis in my work and my life. Without the training I have been privileged to receive, I would not be the person, professional, mother, friend, or wife that I am today.

Through my business relationships, I met David J. Zumpano, who became my personal mentor. An entrepreneur, CPA, and attorney, Dave was my personal coach for more than five years. When his training organization, MPS, LLC, began to grow, he invited me to lead his team, which I continue to do today. In 2007, I became CEO/Director of Member Services/Strategic Planner and Coach of MPS, LLC. I lead a thriving national attorney training organization along with my cutting-edge company, which is dedicated to creating, training, and supporting "intrapreneurs" in an entrepreneur's world. I manage budgets, serve as a Professional Accountability Implementation Nag (PAIN), create marketing campaigns, and develop strategic alliances, and everything else required when running a successful business on a daily basis. But my true passion is business coaching, and I have worked with more than three hundred law firms in this capacity. I love what I do, and I am committed to making a difference at work and at home in Parker, CO, where I live with my husband Shaun and our spirited children, Aidan Patrick, seven; and Ella Ryan, four.

Note from Laney Lyons

I worked for 12 years in an estate and business planning law firm for a very entrepreneurial attorney, where I landed after a brief stint in the Army. I had just turned 21 and had been released from boot camp with a knee injury, so I began temping for a law firm as a receptionist, which turned into my permanent job. Though I had completed high school and a few semesters of college, I had no degree and no real office experience at all. I didn't even know what "dress code" meant, and I really needed a refresher course on my grammar, but I always had that "do it right or not at all" quality, and luckily, my boss recognized a diamond in the rough. I had that same quality every hiring manager looks for when hiring–that "bring it on, I can do it!" attitude.

Now, 12 years later, I have helped create business models and license them to other law firms. I train attorneys and their teams across the country. I've co-led a national key assistant program, teaching many of the techniques we will share with you in this book. I've co-authored a book published by Simon & Schuster. I've learned to hire, fire, and manage my team, and I've started a successful business of my own.

But that's just what I've *done*. What I've *become* is much more astounding to me. I went from the Army to a temp agency with no real goals in life. At 21, I felt I had already used up too many options. I felt embarrassed about my lack of progress and was pretty mad at myself because I knew I was smart, yet I had put myself on a path to nowhere special. I knew this aimlessness wasn't for me. I needed a place to make a difference. I needed a game to play–a game I could *win*. I also needed a team of people I respected to play the game with me. And I found it. Today I have the privilege of making a difference for key assistants I train and being a role model to young women in my family.

In 2009, I felt heartbroken while watching so many attorneys I knew struggle to keep their firms alive during the economic downturn. So, I created Your Outsource Resource, LLC, as an outsourcing solution to attorneys who need estate planning drafting and funding services.

A few weeks after launching the company, I journeyed to Cambodia on a volunteer trip. I fell in love with this country and its sweet, hard-working children. And I plan to return each year to the orphanage to teach and continually remind these children how special they are.

The most important thing I've learned along the way is that success doesn't come by clocking in and clocking out. It comes from dedicated attention, taking control of your job, and making it what you want it to be. But it's not an everyday "high" by any means—rarely do I wake up and say, "Yep, today I have the time and energy to take that job by the horns." It happens slowly, and on the worst days, you may want to chuck it all. But if you hold your ground and push forward, you'll get there. After all, it's the rest of your life. Isn't it worth it?

CHAPTER 1

Entitled Chick

Dumping Your Entitlement Mentality

"When a milestone is conquered, the subtle erosion called 'entitlement' begins its consuming grind. The team regards its greatness as a trait and a right. Half-hearted effort becomes habit and saps a champion."

- Pat Riley

What turns a good employee into a great one? What transforms a job into a career? What makes some people successful, despite their lack of education, experience, or training? If you could learn one thing that would give you the power to go from good to great, to turn your job into a career, and to outperform those with even more education, experience, and training, how much value would you place on such an invaluable lesson? What difference would that make in your life?

In this chapter, we'll share the most important concept that you need to know in order to succeed when working for a small business. It won't cost thousands of dollars in schooling, and it won't take years to learn. It simply takes an open mind and the courage to take an honest look at yourself and consider how you think about your job and your life.

This concept is critical to your success when working with an entrepreneur. Mastering this ability to recognize and understand why you react in certain ways at work will be the difference between picking up a few tips and being a foundation for your unlimited personal and career growth. The good news is that it doesn't actually require you to do much of anything. Once you understand the concept, it's like sharpening the focus on a camera—everything becomes clearer. The bad news is that it requires you to think "bigger," drop any preconceived notions, and act more like a business owner. Once you see things clearly, we promise that your world will never be the same again.

The Secret Concept

So what is this elusive concept that can make such a difference in your life and career? Very simply, it's getting rid of your Entitlement Mentality. Ask yourself the following questions and see if any strike a chord with you:

- Are you generally a helpful person?
- Do you mind staying a bit late to help a colleague finish a job or meet a deadline?
- Do you often have numerous tasks that require you to work overtime to complete them in a timely fashion?
- Do you usually complete tasks on time, or do you ask yourself why you're staying late to finish up, when your boss is leaving right on time to get home to his family? (After all, you have a family, too!)

- Do you feel like you are doing all the work, but your boss is getting paid for it?

Laney remembers one time thinking, "I am usually pretty down-to-earth and naturally jump in and do whatever I need to do in order to keep the office running smoothly, without being asked. It's no big deal to me because it helps me deal with my own workload. I feel like being a team player is one of my strengths. But one day I started to feel a bit of resentment, even though I wholeheartedly believe in being a team player. Why? When my boss asked if I could get him a cup of coffee so he could continue working on a current project, a little voice deep inside me said, "Sure! Like I don't have plenty of work I need to do, too!"

I began to feel guilty, and even questioned myself. I starting asking, "Where did my drive go? Why do I feel bitter over little things that never bothered me before?"

I'm the one who supports my co-workers and makes sure they get credit with the boss. Why, then, did I begin comparing the hours they work with my own? I usually defended them! I thought maybe I was just going through a phase, or that I was a little burned out and needed a little time off.

To be honest, I was slowly starting to think, "Just give me my paycheck, please!"

Has this happened to you? If you once had passion for your job, but now find yourself just going through the motions, read on. If you used to think you could accomplish anything, but now doubt yourself, or worse, doubt your boss, please, keep reading. Or, if you never really had a particular fire, passion, or vision for a job at all, this book is for you.

The most important thing to remember when these nasty little thoughts start popping up is that *it's not you*! It's just your *reaction* to the chaos, constant change and pace of working with an entrepreneur. *Your defense mechanism kicks in when the realities of day-to-day life in a small business are inconsistent with the hopes you had when you accepted your position.* It's the sneaky onset of what we call "entitlement."

Merriam Webster's Definition of Entitlement

The belief that one is deserving of or entitled to certain privileges.

Our Definition of Entitlement

When the things you used to appreciate about your job become things you begin to expect;

when privileges no longer seem like privileges, but expectations; and when you have lost any sense of appreciation and gratitude. When you don't see that the opportunity to grow is an opportunity someone has given you, and for which you must work hard to attain and maintain, you feel entitled. When you see an opportunity as something you expect to be given to you, no matter how big or small your effort and accomplishment, you feel entitled.

Why is the "Entitlement Mentality" Harmful?

You might be asking yourself the following questions:

- What's the harm in indulging in a few of these thoughts?
- What's the downside to blowing off a little steam?

You still do your job—better than most, in fact. There may be nothing "wrong" with your reactions. But being "right" may not allow you to obtain the potential growth, increased pay, and success that you desire.

If you're working in a small business, you're working for an entrepreneur.

Merriam Webster's Definition of Entrepreneur

One who organizes, manages, and assumes the risks of a business or enterprise

Our Definition of Entrepreneur

An innovative business owner who is full of never-ending ideas and possibilities who may cause chaos wherever he or she goes, but also creates opportunities and new perspectives.

The Entrepreneurial Environment

Working in an entrepreneurial environment is different from working in a big organization, largely due to the inconsistent rules. *In a small business, you usually have to "earn" your respect and pay, as opposed to putting in enough hours and years to accumulate title and pay raises.* Things change rapidly, sometimes hour to hour. In large companies, things change much more slowly, because there are more channels to go through.

However, working for an entrepreneur usually comes with a tremendous amount of opportunity. You're usually involved in projects that wouldn't come your way in most large companies. You share in the excitement of participating in the growing of a business. You usually have the opportunity to work on a team and you can eventually learn how to build and lead one. You get to work hand-in-hand with the entrepreneur, whereas in a large company, you probably never speak two words to the business owner. A wealth of information and experience passes by your ears daily, if you listen for it. You can earn a "real-world business degree," which you can't earn in school, and you are rewarded based on your results and the value you bring to the company, not on your education level. The possibilities are endless.

A small business is a combination of glamour and the downright dingy. It is a small, non-corporate, entrepreneurial environment where many opportunities are available, but you must dig in and get your hands dirty to succeed. In an entrepreneurial environment, one moment you can be on stage teaching millionaires how to protect their wealth, and the next moment you might be cleaning out the trash in the bathroom. Working in a small business can be very detail-oriented, but you also can see the dynamics of a larger organization amid those details. In a small business, you see the forest *and* the trees.

Working in a small business also means that you're in the business of change. Most small businesses don't have the financial cushion that large companies have, and aren't backed by government funds. They must be profitable to survive. This means that they must be able to change direction on a dime and offer new products and services when demand for their current services lessens. Working in a small business also means you must accept, deal with, and even embrace change. Change happening in small businesses is more a matter of *when*–not *if*.

Merriam Webster's Definition of Change

1. *To make different in some particular:* ALTER
2. *To make radically different:* TRANSFORM
3. *To give a different position, course, or direction*

Our Definition of Change

I left work yesterday as the administrative assistant for a company that sells mortgages. When I arrived at work this morning, I was the salesperson for a company that leases office space!

The Importance of Providing Value

Earlier, we said that being "right" regarding your frustrations about constant changes, having to work on tasks below your qualifications, and other annoying things might not bring you the success you desire. But just as a small business must make a profit to survive, you must be *valuable* to the company to survive, as well. Maybe you're very valuable right now, but if you begin looking through the lens of "being right" all the time, you will quickly lose your ability to see what value you're producing for the business.

You can be "right" about your treatment at work, but your boss won't keep paying you for being right. Business owners can only afford to pay you to be valuable to their company. If they paid people for being right, they would go out of business, and none of us would have jobs.

The Two Rules of Survival

Have you ever worked with someone who came into work every day as a force to be reckoned with–someone who learned quickly, worked hard, and someone you were thrilled to have on your team?

Have you ever noticed this same person suddenly change and become a complainer all the time? Maybe she started spending more time worrying about when you came in and how long you took for lunch instead of focusing on her own work, for example. This person has what we call "Entitlement Mentality." She's forgotten to measure success based on the results that her team members are producing. Instead, she compares her team to herself in a way in which she feels insulted and unappreciated. She stops appreciating that you helped the company land a huge new account that will contribute greatly to its profits that year (which means that everyone will get bigger Christmas bonuses). Instead, she's complaining that you were 30 minutes late on Tuesday and that she had to take your phone calls to cover for you.

This sense of entitlement is a slippery slope, because those who fall victim to it are usually those with the most potential in a company. They start out as all-star players but then fall into a mentality of comparing and measuring their colleagues vs. themselves.

If this has happened to you, read carefully. You may be right regarding some of your feelings, but there's a better way to overcome these feelings than developing a mindset of entitlement. Remember, you're working to produce value in a small business, so find a way to address your aggravations in a way that reduces your stress and frustration, but also produces value to your entrepreneur. Often, as a key employee, your workload continually increases. Because you're smart, a hard worker, and can be trusted, you're given increasing responsibility until you're drowning in work. As a reaction, you get fed up, go to your boss, and plead with him to hire someone to assist you so that you can get more work accomplished.

This is the biggest faux pas you can make. Some of you may have been in this position before and felt surprised by your boss's response that "I am drowning in work, too, and I can't afford to hire a new employee right now." At this point, it's very easy for a small seed of bitterness to creep into your mind and grow like a tangled weed into your business environment.

Were you wrong to ask for extra help? Absolutely not. Is there perhaps a better way you could have positioned your request? Absolutely. Rather than pleading for someone to help you because you can't keep working late every night and you're stressed to the max, you should reposition your request to focus on ways to help the company profit and increase the value you bring to the company.

Don't turn your request into something that the business owner hears as costing him money; instead, transform it into something that will *make* money for him. For instance, you could say, "How do you feel about hiring someone else in support staff to help us increase the profits here?"

Take a look at this scenario, for example:

Goal

Find a way to open five hours a week of the business owner's time to do additional marketing and sales work. If he had five more hours per week, he could conduct three more face-to-face sales meetings. Then suppose that each meeting is a potential $8,000 in income to the company. If the business owner has a 50 percent closing ratio, he would close one new client each week, which could equal an extra $32,000 a month.

Plan

Let's say that currently, the business owner spends approximately five hours weekly entering sales meeting notes into the contact's file, sending follow-up information, and scheduling follow-up meetings to close a deal. If you can persuade him to dictate the sales meeting notes to you, train you to input those notes into the contact's file, mail information, and schedule follow-up reminders on his calendar, you could also persuade him to hire a part-time receptionist, which will cost less than $32,000 a year, even after benefits. Show him your goal of $32,000 extra per month, which, if he hired a part-time receptionist, would cost less than the additional income the company would make in one *month*.

Action

Create a structure in which you can "try this on" for 30 days. Then, stipulate that if you can prove to your boss that you can generate $32,000 of additional revenue in 30 days, you will earn a two-percent bonus of $640. Not bad, right?

This proposal will address your frustration at having to constantly answer the phones while trying to work on the more important things that you have to do. It will also free you from your "overqualified" receptionist position. Also, the business owner will see the plan as a great way to help the company grow. It follows our rule of "the company must profit to survive." It also follows the second part of the rule, that "you must produce value to survive."

This proposal isn't just about you asking for something. It shows how giving you what you ask for will allow you to continue to produce more value for the business owner, which translates into dollars—thousands of them! It's a win-win situation for everyone.

Were you wrong to feel frustrated about being overworked? No. Did you find a better way to address your frustration that shows your business savvy and gives you an opportunity to grow in the company while making more money for it? Yes. To continually grow, you must learn to push away the Entitlement Mentality and find solutions that work for you *and* the company.

The Roots of Entitlement Mentality

Think back to your own childhood. Without knowing it, you learned a lot from what you heard your parents say. But your parents lived and worked in a different time than you do now. Unless they were business owners, most people in your parents' generation wanted to obtain seniority at a job, probably at a large corporation or government agency, where they could earn a pension and have stability and benefits. In those types of work environments, solid years on the job played a large part in promotions. There were a lot of rules, and protocol was the order of the day. It was easy for someone to be "wronged" or treated "unfairly" if the rules weren't followed. Our parents focused on the short-term rewards, such as getting promotions, and on the long-term rewards of putting in enough years to retire comfortably and draw their pensions.

In today's world, there are no pensions, especially in an entrepreneurial environment. Small businesses must profit to survive, and if you work for a small business, you must create value to survive within it. This erases all "lines" for promotion, and renders "years of service" irrelevant, unless you're growing each year *with* the company.

We are living in the age of the entrepreneur. According to the U.S. Department of State approximately "19.6 million Americans work for companies employing fewer than 20 workers, and 18.4 million work for firms employing between 20 and 99 workers." The business owner is king of his own kingdom. We must equip ourselves with a different way of thinking that will fit our time and set the standard for our children, after us. We must learn to work with new rules.

To win this game, we're no longer evaluated by the hours or years worked. We're measured by what we contribute to the small businesses for which we work, the entrepreneur's quality of life, and ultimately, the value we create in our own world. It's easy to rationalize giving ourselves what we want by believing we're the only ones taking a risk helping the business grow or keeping it healthy. We forget that everyone who ties his or her future to the entrepreneur's vision is risking something—earning potential, reputation, career security, or other professional opportunities.

Techniques for Your Day-to-Day Life

Now that you understand entitlement and how it can erode your best efforts in an organization, let's discuss how to catch it when it creeps into your daily life.

It's easy for even the best of us to slip into Entitlement Mentality, and nothing threatens the entrepreneurial force of a business owner more. Also, nothing annoys a business owner more than hearing something like, "When Camille was in my position, she made more than me…"

Here is Molly's story – living proof of what *not* to do:

I had been working for an entrepreneur for one year, I agreed to leave my former employer for the same base salary with the potential to double that income in quarterly bonuses by working for him. A year later, I didn't get a single bonus. Therefore, I decided that it was time for a "talk" with the boss. I spent two solid weeks crafting a four-page proposal, including:

- *My current role.*

- *What I had taken on/become accountable for since I had started.*

- *The things I expected to accomplish in the next year.*

- *The things I wanted to accomplish over the next 90 days.*

- *The things I would require to be satisfied with my progress in the job in one year.*

- *My current compensation.*

- *My suggestions for a structure for short-term and long-term compensation.*

- *What I'm getting out of being here other than a paycheck.*

As he was reading and got to the part where I thought I had cleverly laid out my "current compensation," he read aloud, "I'm currently making double that as a base salary, but the CEO I replaced was earning 2.2X."

My boss couldn't believe it. "Hold the phone," he said. "Are you kidding me? You really can't mean this."

At that point, all I could think was, "Oh no, I'm not getting my raise."

I thought that I was entitled to make at least half the amount of the previous CEO; it's a win-win situation, right? But I hadn't considered my boss's perspective.

He explained that when he hired the previous CEO, he had no business plan. He had no frame of reference regarding what worked and what didn't work, and what specific, measurable results he wanted him to accomplish. When he was buried with work and stressed to the end of his rope, the CEO was the first person who crossed his path. He wanted the pain to go away, and he didn't care what it cost to make that happen.

But since he had hired me, he had been running this place like a business and had a great team in place. He learned a lot from his lesson.

I totally missed the boat. Yes, I had created two times the value of my salary and deserved my raise. But I was approaching my proposal from a place of entitlement (I am entitled to make at least half what the last CEO made), not value creation (I am creating value to support the raise I am requesting). My intentions were good, but my delivery was horrific. I also missed the point that the last CEO may have made more than me, but he also wasn't there anymore! If I had approached it from a place of value creation and taken my boss's perspective into account, I would have said it differently, and it would have been received in a much more positive light.

Entitlement Checklist

In an effort to support (and save) you, we've created a checklist for you to use when you feel yourself getting frustrated or bitter. This will help you see if you need to reposition your requests and responses. Again, you may be "right" in your thinking, but this checklist will help you determine if Entitlement Mentality has crept into your thinking and verbiage. You may need to reposition yourself before you approach your boss so that you can communicate the value you produce, and not just be seen as a whiner.

Here's the golden rule for asking for something: *Don't present a problem unless you have a proposed solution.*

This is a wonderful "check-in place" to determine if you're operating from a place of entitlement:

1. Clarify what my boss asked me to do, and explain what stands in the way of taking on that task.

2. Check that my intentions are best for the business as a whole, not just for my own personal gain.

3. Clarify my vision for achieving this goal.

4. What are the emotional potholes for me in this conversation that I should avoid?

5. How can I avoid these potholes?

6. What am I putting on the line to resolve this matter? Is it worth it?

7. What am I specifically requesting of my boss?

8. What does my boss have to do to commit to achieve the next action?

9. Do I need anyone else's feedback/support before I approach my boss?

These questions will help you stay focused on the facts and what you want to achieve for the business and yourself, and not slip into "well because" (a big, red flag you are slipping into entitlement).

The Stockdale Paradox

| Retain faith that you will prevail in the end, regardless of the difficulties. | AND at the same time | Confront the most brutal facts of your current reality, whatever they might be. |

Don't Be a Yes Chick Action Plan: Complete the entitlement checklist, watch your language, take action steps to change any entitlement thinking, and seek support when needed.

CHAPTER 2

Passionate Chick

Find Passion and Fulfillment

*"When work, commitment, and pleasure
all become one and you reach that deep well
where passion lives, nothing is impossible."*

- Nancy Coey

W hat motivates people to do, well… *anything?*

That is the million-dollar question that business owners, consultants, and management gurus have been asking since the day that the guy who invented the wheel started hiring people to make and sell wheels.

Business owners pay motivational speakers a handsome sum of money at conference centers all over the world to come in and motivate the troops, even though extensive research has shown that you can't really motivate another person, at least not for any extended length of time. You can dangle carrots and wield sticks that will have short-term effects or that will appeal to an individual's susceptibility to greed or fear, and you can even inspire his higher nature, but even these motivators will work less and less effectively as time moves on.

You may not be able to motivate someone else, but you can discover what motivates *you.* Moreover, you can use that awareness as a key to unlock all the latent creative talents and passion within yourself. Intrinsic motivation that comes from the inside out is the only lasting passion that will be there day after day, and won't need a constant stream of reminders, nudges, encouragement, threats, and bribes to maintain.

As an **intrapreneur** (a person who works for an entrepreneur, typically in a small business atmosphere, who takes direct responsibility and accountability for thinking like a business owner about how to run and grow the company through assertive risk-taking and innovation) you must find that internal passion, but part of your role is also to help your team find the passion within themselves.

How do you find this hidden motivational switch? What inspires one person to do her job with passion, while another equally gifted person may perform the same task begrudgingly or mechanically, doing only the minimum required to get by? Why is one person inspired to do one particular task, but not inspired about another task? You spend at least eight to nine hours a day at your job—almost 25 to 30 percent of your life. If you're a clock-watchin' kind of gal, you're missing something really important in your work life—passion.

Sadly, many people don't enjoy their work. Worse still, they have no expectation that they should. They simply show up for work, look busy, and collect a paycheck to pay the bills in order to live–and work. Is it any wonder why most heart attacks and strokes in America take place on Monday mornings, as people begrudgingly ready themselves for another week of unfulfilling labor?

Being passionate about your job is more than the old cliché, "Do what you love." It's about looking *forward* to going to work. It's looking at the clock at 2 p.m. and realizing that you never took your morning bagel out of the toaster. It's working past "quitting" time, not because you're swamped with work, but because you're so involved that you don't notice time. Is this the reality of *your* world?

If you're not passionate about your work, you may feel like you're just going through the motions, and wondering if this is all your life has to offer. You may be asking yourself, "What happened to my dreams?" If your life is currently full of passion, this chapter will help you identify the traits that contribute to it so that you'll always have the tools to mend your confidence when it gets low or when you need a reminder of why you do what you do day in and day out. If your life isn't driven by your passion now, keep reading, and you'll learn to identify what you're passionate about and find some simple ways to restructure the "stuff" in your life so that it feeds your desires.

If you are afraid of "finding your passion" because it involves running off to Paris, Pisa, or Prague to study art and history, or quitting your job to become a pianist, or something else that may disappoint those around you, rest easy. This chapter will help you find your passion whether you're in Des Moines, Detroit, or Dayton. Even if you chucked this life and ran off to something more aligned with your fantasies, chances are that if you don't know how to identify the key elements of that passion, you'd quickly find yourself exactly where you are now, but without a steady paycheck.

Merriam Webster's Definition of Passion

1. *Intense, driving, or overmastering feeling or conviction*
2. *A strong liking or desire for or devotion to some activity, object, or concept*

Our Definition of Passion

Having knowledge of the following:

1. *Exactly what your next day will look like;*
2. *The top three things that you're going to knock out of the ballpark;*
3. *Knowing you're X amount of dollars away from making your monthly revenue goal (i.e., having money in your pocket), and looking forward to getting up tomorrow.*

Your Unique Ability®[1]

Where are *you* great? What's unique about your own constellation of gifts? What do you enjoy doing the most? What comes naturally for you? Finding the answers to these questions will help you discover your unique collection of strengths—your own Unique Ability®. Unique Ability is a concept created by Dan Sullivan, founder of The Strategic Coach®. Unique Ability is a combination of your personal talents, passions, and skills. When you begin to figure out this important foundation of who you are, you'll understand what you do best in life, and what you love doing most.

There's a good chance that you've already taken a variety of assessment tools to determine your psychological type, cognitive intelligence, social style, or emotional intelligence. Usually, you're presented with a "holistic" picture of your strengths and weaknesses. Then, you're given a prescription to help you shore up your weaknesses and learn how to flex your less-dominant modes of perception, social style, or communication preferences.

It's definitely good to know your weaknesses, but it's not good to spend all your time, attention, and energy compulsively shoring them up.

The key to finding your intrinsic motivation and using it to energize your passion at work is to not only know your strengths, but to *focus on them*.

One way of solving this mystery it is to look at what actions energize you. Not only do you have a talent for something, but doing this "something" rejuvenates you rather than depletes you. That "something" is your "Unique Ability." Often, this Unique Ability is invisible to you. You do it so effortlessly that you don't even notice it. You even have trouble recognizing its value. But others don't. Your Unique Ability is just second nature to you. *The secret to a passionate life is to turn your second nature into your primary revenue stream.*

To begin discovering your Unique Ability, ask yourself the following:

- "What actions or projects do others most often compliment me on?" "Do I see a pattern concerning these expressions of appreciation, gratitude, and acknowledgment?"
- "What activities make me forget about time?"[1]

---

1. Unique Ability® is a registered trademark, protected by copyright and an integral part of The Strategic Coach, Inc. All rights reserved. Used with written permission. For more information, please visit www.strategiccoach.com.

Sometimes, you won't always know the answers to these questions, so we suggest that you do the following "Unique Ability" exercise (from the book *Unique Ability: Creating the Life You Want*). Conduct your own personal poll of 10 to 20 people in your circle of influence. Include both personal and professional contacts in order to receive a well-rounded perspective. Ask them the following questions:

- "What activities do I do well?"
- "Where do I have endless commitment and passion in my life?"

You'll discover that a common, unambiguous response will ring out crystal clear. That will be your Unique Ability.

Using Your Unique Ability

Once you discover your special talent, you must learn how to honor it. As an intrapreneur, it will be a balancing act that you'll have to continually monitor. There will always be certain tasks that you'll be required to perform that you're not good at, or that you dislike. But, as the responsible team player that you are, you'll be tempted to force yourself to do it for the company. You'll just suck it up and take one for the team. That's all well and good on occasion, but remember to monitor your feelings and moods as you do these non-Unique Ability tasks so that you don't lose your passion, energy, good humor, momentum, and productivity. Know your own limits. If you keep saying "yes!" to every one of these tasks because you're a born do-gooder and team player, you'll end up spending 80, 90, or 100 percent of your workday engaged in non-Unique Ability work, and you'll grow to hate the job you once loved and wonder why you're going home from work exhausted.

Business owners want their people who use their unique abilities and are in touch with their passion at least 70 percent of the time. If people spend more than 30 percent of their time at work doing tasks that don't fully engage them, they'll always be trolling for a better job. They'll have Monster.com bookmarked, and will offer themselves to the highest bidders. Their bodies may be at the office every day, but their hearts, minds, and souls will be elsewhere. They'll start to see themselves more like "hired hands," and those idle hands will go walking through the Yellow Pages for a more attractive job where they can use their unique abilities.

On the flip side, people who spend 70 percent or more of their time at work engaged in their passion tend to remain loyal to that workplace. Money can't tempt them. They're intrinsically motivated, and *extrinsic* motivation (more money) won't be enough to get them to go somewhere else.

The Best $49.95 You'll Ever Spend!

Wouldn't it be great if there were a methodology that could guide you to the career that would let you be true to yourself by helping you apply your innate abilities to a business?

The Kolbe Wisdom™ is a series of assessment tools developed by educator Kathy Kolbe that tests your conative abilities, or creative instincts. "Conative" defines the mental processes or behaviors directed towards action or change, and include impulse, volition, and desire. It's not what you think or what you feel, but rather your "will," or your instincts.

The Kolbe A™ Index is neither a personality nor an intelligence test. It simply gauges how you instinctively react to a situation or a problem and gives you an understanding of your innate MO (*modus operandi*), or how you operate. Your MO governs your actions, reactions, and interactions. It also determines how you communicate and prefer to use your time. Once you understand your MO, you're free to be your authentic self and operate according to your unique method of doing things.

Why is this important? When you're not being your authentic self, you allow other people or circumstances to interfere with your instinctive energy. Your effectiveness will then be reduced, and you'll experience stress. You may become weak and "out of tune," and not function optimally in the workplace.

Furthermore, by using the Kolbe method, both individual and team performance can be predicted with great accuracy via comparisons of instinctive realities, self-expectations, and requirements.

There are four Kolbe Action Modes®:

- Fact Finder – Fact Finder behavior is the instinctive way we gather and share information

- Follow Thru – Follow Thru behavior is the instinctive way we arrange and design

- Quick Start – Quick Start behavior is the instinctive way we deal with risk and uncertainty

- Implementor – Implementor behavior is the instinctive way we handle space and tangibles

Here's how these different Kolbe types would respond to the same stimulus. Let's say that you fill a paper bag with several household items like paperclips, string, rubber bands, etc. You then take a person of each Kolbe type and present her with the following hypothetical situation: "You work for a toy company and have 30 minutes to design a new toy for the Christmas holidays."

The initiating *Fact Finder* will say, "What's the target age group? How much will it cost? What should it do?" She will naturally be the first to ask questions, because she needs facts to operate comfortably.

The initiating *Follow Thru* will take all the items in the paper bag, organize them into separate groups, and then figure out a plan to create and build a new toy. She needs to understand exactly what's being asked of her. She will thoroughly prepare herself and avoid last-minute and sudden changes. Some people refer to this type of person as a "professional nag." She's the entrepreneur's safety net. For instance, a Quick Start may make a lot of promises to clients and vendors without knowing whether she can actually deliver on them. The Follow Thru will work hard to ensure that she meets these promises.

The initiating *Quick Start* will tend to jump in and start putting all the items in the bag together, seeing what fits and what doesn't, without remembering what she's trying to accomplish. She's comfortable with experimenting and improvising. A "quick start" works well under pressure, or when the situation is ambiguous or dicey. The downside of this MO is that she may rush to the completion stage too early, before having all the facts, and end up having to redo what the team has already put together.

The initiating *Implementer* will put her hands on the clips and the string and begin building something. She's the person most likely to need plenty of props and prototypes to perform her job. This Kolbe type will likely find her passion as a contractor, or maybe an artist.

The ultimate key is to "know thyself" while respecting your teammates' MOs. In most cases, it takes all four Kolbes to make an effective, well-rounded team. You can discover your Kolbe type by visiting the website at **www.kolbe.com**. The Kolbe A Index costs $49.95, and it will be the best $49.95 you'll ever spend!

Team Kolbe

As an entrepreneur, you want to build a team that can take advantage of a mix of MOs. When a team is functioning at a high level, you can truly say that the whole is greater than the sum of its parts. Finding and hiring people with complementary strengths is building your "Unique Ability® Team."

The most productive part of using the Kolbe assessment is to find other people who really excel in areas where you are weak. That way, you get the most out of your team. It wouldn't make sense to surround yourself with people who have your same strengths and weaknesses. You want your team to consist of people who have complementary strengths, who are dramatically different from you in their skill sets, thinking, and motivational make-up.

If you like thinking big and creating new products and services, for example, but are lousy at promoting, marketing, and selling these new products and services, hire someone who has a passion and motivation for selling and marketing to be on your team. If you're very creative, but lack organizational skills, hire someone who has a passion for order to do this for you. It's that simple.

The key is to know who you are and choose to work in positions that feed your passion; otherwise, you might encounter undue stress and low job satisfaction if you are working too hard to be something you are not.

Finding an Appropriate Work Environment

The best entrepreneur to work for is someone who has developed a business that he's passionate about—who's doing what he loves—or someone who has found a way to express his passion.

The ideal workplace is one where you feel that you make a difference to others and know that you are accomplishing something worthwhile while maintaining some control over your future.

A good example of this kind of person is our friend, Jennifer, who's an attorney. She's not really that passionate about law; that alone doesn't motivate or rejuvenate her. However, through her law practice, she has found a way to teach and coach other people, and *that* brings out her passion and inspires the team.

A different example is another lawyer friend, a hip young guy named Mark, who has always had a passion for gardening and enjoys working with that which is pure, holistic, organic, and outdoorsy, while helping others. This is consistent with his work as an estate and elder law attorney. Many lawyers gravitate towards that specialty because they get their "high" from helping people rather than winning that big courtroom case.

Mark had lost his passion for the business of law. He knew there was something missing in his life, but he couldn't pinpoint it, so he enrolled in the "Passion Quest" program offered by Steve Riley, an attorney and coach. Through his work in this life-changing course, Mark created a new business called "Prodigal Farm," where he helps homeless men and those coming out of drug and rehab therapy to return to and function in society. They come to his farm and help him work, using their hands as part of their therapy. Ironically, since he founded this organization, his law firm has taken off and he's doubled his revenue.

Finding Your Passion

What does passion at work look like?

If you serve in a support role for an entrepreneur, you may or may not be working in the industry or exact field of your passion. It may not be practical for you to immediately quit your job and start all over in a whole new industry, as most of us have financial and personal responsibilities. Due to this situation, many continue to labor in passionless jobs because the work isn't that hard, the people are sometimes fun, and the benefits are good. However, it is possible to find passion *within* a job.

If you get honest with yourself, you probably aren't exactly sure what you're passionate about. There may be a lot of things you enjoy doing, but you've been so busy serving as a good employee that you may have lost touch with your exact passion. Perhaps you have never known what that passion is. Most people want to feel like they make a difference at work, that they help the world become a better place by helping another person or creating something beautiful to inspire others. You may not be a doctor, a teacher, or an artist, but you can create that feeling in your job. It's there already; you just haven't seen it yet.

How to Get Passionate About Your Work:

1. Surround yourself with the right people.

The job of your dreams, straight from the page of your passion, can be unfulfilling if you aren't surrounded by the right people. These are the ones who not only call you to be the best that you can be, but refuse to let you be any less. The right people don't let you sell yourself short. They believe in you and encourage you to believe in yourself. They may be mentors or role models, or you may be in a leadership position to them. These people don't expect perfection from you, but they do expect greatness over the long run. No flame of passion can ignite or continue to burn in a vacuum. A workplace full of negative, passionless, and going-through-the-motions people is toxic. Like a vampire, it will suck out any passion that you have.

2. Get your life priorities straight.

The "big rocks" in your life are the things you love. Such as your family members or outside passions, and your job should support them. Does your work environment allow you the flexibility to take time off to attend your child's school functions? Or, if your big rock is traveling around the world, does your job allow you to take three weeks off at a time to travel to faraway places? Maybe your job isn't your "passion," but it can allow you the opportunity to comfortably enjoy the passions you do have in life.

3. Open the toolbox.

To be passionate, you not only understand what you're doing, but you have confidence in it as well. If you don't have all the tools and resources you need to get your job done, ask for training. Be a lifetime learner and enroll in a "passion-feeding" educational event every quarter. Commit to one new workshop outside of work to expand your toolbox. Whether it's a communication class, a technology workshop, or simply attending a two-hour speaking engagement by an author who inspires you, it will enliven your passion.

4. Enlist others' support.

Discover what motivates you. If you can't do this on your own, ask for help from those around you whom you trust and admire. It may be the last person you would expect, or even someone who intimidates you.

Here's a story from Laney that serves as a good example of this scenario:

I had been working at a law firm for four years, and I liked my job. I worked with people who encouraged me, pushed me to grow, and helped me develop self-confidence. I had the training, resources, and knowledge to do a good job. I started thinking about growing further in this same workplace I loved so much, and I began to seriously consider attending law school to become an attorney. That achievement would have allowed me to have unending growth in my current workplace with more responsibility and more money. I shared my desires with my boss. He had already been very supportive of me going to school, so I knew that wasn't a problem. But I wanted his opinion. Would I make a good attorney and what would it mean for my growth opportunities at the firm? He answered with one simple question of his own: "What do you love about your job?" That was a hard question. I loved my co-workers, and my work was a lot of fun. But I had to think, what was it exactly that I loved about my work?

"I love talking to our clients," I answered. "I love hearing about their lives, especially their kids. When we discuss estate plans, they tell us about all their hopes and dreams for their children, and you can see their eyes light up. You get to hear about their children's accomplishments. You get to hear how the husbands and wives met each other, and all the wonderful, even heartbreaking events that they've shared together. Every time I talk to a client, it's not just about a document they want or a legal question they need answered; I hear the love they have for their children, spouse, or community."

My boss wisely answered me. "You don't need to be an attorney to do that," he said.

He went on to advise me that if I had answered that I loved the law, the research, and the technical and legal aspects, he would have wholeheartedly encouraged me to go to law school. But I didn't need to go to law school to hear the clients' stories and to help ensure that their estate planning wishes were carried out. Since then, I've moved more and more into working directly with clients and prospective clients of our firm. In fact, they like that I'm not an attorney. I'm a layperson, just like them, talking to them about how planning can help them and their families, and why our firm is the team they should use. I employ the skills I enjoy, like writing, public speaking, and event planning. I help write books, newsletters, and marketing materials for the firm. And I get to plan parties and conferences. One of the fundamental keys to unlocking my passion—making a difference for the aging population and their children—has been fulfilled. I talk mostly with elderly people—whom I genuinely enjoy and learn from—about helping their children or grandchildren grow up to be successful, loving people. Through my clients, I help make a difference in the world.

By being asked the right questions and by not just following the logical next step to a bigger paycheck, I found some keys to my passion, and they were right in front of me! And as I grew, rather than being molded by my job, I expanded my job description to include skills I enjoyed, like writing and public speaking.

Now, many years after that crossroads, I've made a difference by helping the community, like organizing golf tournaments to benefit the educational needs of underprivileged children, and taking my first trip to Cambodia to volunteer with children and seniors disabled by polio and landmine explosions. If I had gone to law school as the next logical step in my career path, who knows if I would have found my passion? Maybe I would never have really looked for it, thinking I had made a right career choice. I may have "followed the job" rather than making the job follow me.

Now, don't go into the office tomorrow and say, "I don't like that we sell computer services, because I'm not passionate about it." Take responsibility for how you communicate. Laney loves to teach, but who could see that as a possibility in a law firm? At first, it may have seemed as though she would have to quit, but she found a way to teach—she teaches the team and the attorneys by training them on the firm's systems and processes. Even at the law firm, she found a way to express her passion. She didn't need to leave to fulfill her dreams—everything she needed was right there.

Locating Your Passion Keys

1. What do you enjoy most about your job?

_____

_____

_____

2. *Why* do you enjoy that activity?

_____

_____

_____

3. What do you hold most valuable in your personal life?

_____

_____

_____

4. What activities do you participate in regularly in your personal life?

_____

_____

_____

6. What underlying "passion key" or fulfillment do you see in the things that you enjoy most at work?

_____

_____

_____

7. What about the things you do voluntarily in your personal life?

_____

_____

_____

8. Why is not having passion in your job harmful?

_____

_____

_____

9. List three things you are potentially missing out on from not being passionate about your work.

1. _____

2. _____

3. _____

Don't be a Yes Chick Action Plan: Locate your passion keys, poll your network to find your Unique Ability, go through the Unique Ability Discovery Process in the book *Unique Ability: Creating the Life You Want*, take the Kolbe Index A, and talk to a trusted friend, colleague, or coach.

CHAPTER 3

Invaluable Chick

How to Always Provide Value

*"If we're growing, we're always going
to be out of our comfort zone."*

- John Maxwell

At one point or another in our lives, we enter the comfort zone—we live with a sense of ease, security, and poise, a place where we've mastered our jobs and our lives, and yet we don't feel challenged anymore!

You drive to work and no longer feel stirred or excited about that idea mentioned in yesterday's meeting. You can pretty much predict what the day will bring, and you can deliver and conquer with your eyes closed. You've been in your current position for X amount of months or years, and you do it damn well. But something is "missing." You meet the days without that butterfly-in-the-belly feeling. You feel neither angst nor excitement about how you are possibly going to get things moving to produce remarkable results.

Welcome to the doorstep of growth. Welcome to the commencement of Replacing Yourself.

But what does this mean? Are you thinking, "I like what I do, and I do it better than anyone else in the office—plus, there really is no one else to take over what I do." This is the greatest mistake we see intrapreneurs make is the traditional "continuation" in the workplace. You're probably saying, "What's wrong with that?" But this behavior is detrimental when companies are looking for a return on their investment or when employees are looking for that annual raise to climb the proverbial ladder. The real problem is that most employees are not aware that when you replace yourself, you step out of your comfort zone, which is important to your growth.

In all honesty, the boss will have no trouble replacing you with someone who accepts and encourages capability, position, and resourcefulness. So either get busy growing or stay busy existing—either way, you have to choose, and yes, existing in a role without growth is a choice.

We are not talking about managing up, delegating, or giving up control. We are talking about reinventing yourself. It's a scary, intimidating, exciting, and challenging place to be; it's the crossroad where you decide to step up and grow, even if it means operating outside of your comfort zone, or hanging out where you are and settling for "okay."

Molly just found herself standing in this very crossroad:

Every year my company conducts a Year-End Planning Retreat, where we shut down the business for an entire day to work on revisiting our company organizational chart and designing our Top 10 Intentional Projects for the year to come. We start the day by going through the company organizational chart, where we outline all the necessary roles and responsibilities needed to meet our goals and objectives to serve our clients. This year, after two hours the exercise was over, and I started feeling a bit "empty." I have worked with these three people in the role of CEO for the past three years. Now, if you have ever worked for a small company, you know the CEO role means you do a little bit of this and a lot of that. My roles ranged from accounting to customer service on any given day, but every client loved me, and I worked tirelessly with compassion, authenticity, and, most days, with a sense of accomplishment.

I found that as we approached the finance part of the org chart, someone else stepped up and said, "It makes the most logical sense for me to take that over to free Molly up to work on relationship building with Power Partners." When it came to event planning, I found myself saying, "It makes more sense for Jenny to handle that while I focus on new relationships." After completing the company organization chart on this early December morning, I realized that I had just "given away" all of my duties! For so many years I took a tremendous amount of pride in the fact that I could "do it all and everyone depended on me." The company of three had grown to a company of five over the past year.

I now found myself feeling empty, nervous, and excited all at the same time. I realized with a bit of a shock that I was in the exact place I needed to be—I had simply replaced myself.

After going through the Organizational Chart, I found one role where I could put myself— marketing. Never in a million, trillion years would I have put myself in marketing! In fact, anytime the word "marketing" came up, I would literally get a bellyache. But finding myself in this place of angst, I knew I was simply filling the role of a connector, cultivator, and nurturer. Oddly, "marketing" was my Unique Ability!

With the new role, I instantly saw how I could do it, and with pride—and passion! My mind was already buzzing about ways to grow and enhance this new position.

The next morning, we scheduled a one-hour team meeting to distinguish all the roles we reinvented for ourselves. Typically, when we reinvent ourselves, we also create the opportunity for others to reinvent themselves as well. As you leave certain job roles behind that you have outgrown, others are ready to step up and grow into them. This process of reinvention is also an important part of retaining quality employees, as they must have the opportunity to grow and be challenged and fulfilled.

We realized we needed to be responsible and create a Transition Schedule to determine our current activities in our current roles, the time it would take to train the new person; and the steps to systematize it.

One hour later we had a transition schedule that would take four complete days to implement. We scheduled out a week, three weeks from that day, to step into our new roles after that four-day transition phase.

The Eight Laws of Replacing Yourself

To effectively replace yourself in your current role, you need to be able to articulate the what, why, and how of your job. In other words, the weekly practice of "replacing yourself" will create a win-win-win (for your boss, you and your replacement), *every single time.*

The Law of System

If you can't give what you are doing to someone else and ask them to follow certain steps to get the same results you did, you aren't living the Law of System. When you go through your transition, it is imperative that every single step, no matter how simple it may seem, is written in such a way so that you can understand it clearly and sequentially. Break it down into small steps and create a checklist. Casual, verbal references to "the way we do things" or hoarding our work so others must come to you to get it doesn't work. We call this "tribal knowledge."

The Law of System not only allows you to "get rid of it" that much quicker, but sets the stage for the next phase when you find yourself "moving on up." Remember, every time you replace yourself, there is someone one step behind you and someone one step ahead of you. If you don't leave good systems in place, you will constantly have to slide back into your old position, and not have time to do a great job at your new one. Also, it's great to use the systems you have created as a vehicle for show and tell when it comes time for annual reviews, pay raise proposals, and new position openings.

The Law of Growth

Stephen Covey calls it Sharpening the Saw, and some call it S.M.A.R.T. We call it The Law of Growth, or replacing yourself. It's best to continually test yourself to determine if you are living in the comfort zone or in the growth zone. Are you feeling challenged, exhausted, and exhilarated at the end of your day? This is the comfort test. This also allows you to show the boss that they are getting the greatest return on their biggest investment: you. Staying on a growth track will show your employer that you're worth every penny and then some, especially when companies are looking for ways to reduce expenses, collapse roles, and reduce staff.

The Law of Accountability

Life is about accountability. If you don't share what you do with the people with whom you work, your chances of action and success decrease considerably. Reporting and tracking what you are doing and sharing it with everyone in the office in an organized manner via weekly meetings and the like will allow you to not only achieve your goals but also create top mental awareness about your accomplishments.

The Law of Communication

Sending e-mails, voicemails, and texts just because it's faster than actually talking with people is not living the Law of Communication. In today's automated, hi-tech, competitive atmosphere. It actually creates more damage and allows us to hide out versus personally connecting and relating with another. The quality of your relationships are directly tied to the quality of your life.

The Law of Revocability

Replacing yourself and creating your new role is not written in stone. Simply "try it on," and if it doesn't fit like you thought it would, it is completely revocable. There is never punishment for stepping up, systematizing, and leading in the workplace. Give yourself permission to try a new position out, and then redesign it if it is not the right fit for you.

The Law of Pride

Having a commitment to being right and declaring to "know it all" will not only halt your livelihood (because it shows that you're uninterested in learning new ideas and approaches), but it will also send red flags to everyone around you that in your world, life is all about you. When you want to replace yourself and train the "new you," you must give acknowledgement, praise, ask questions, and listen to the person's suggestions. Always give credit where credit is due, and never inappropriately take full credit for a positive outcome despite any help or input you've given. Give credit to others' contributions; you'll be seen as team player, a leader, and a driving force to the thriving group. We're not saying you should take a back seat, but make sure to differentiate between bragging and sharing success through project management, system creation, and successful revenue tracking. There is value in sharing your accomplishments as long as you go about it with pride, inspiration, and a spirit of "paying it forward." It *will* come back to you.

The Law of Enrollment

In order to replace yourself, you must enroll others. If you choose to "do it all," *you will* fail. Your boss doesn't have time to keep a running tab on each employee, so how else will he know how valuable you are to the company unless you tell him? Again, bravado is one thing, but letting colleagues in your industry know of your success through case studies, promotion bulletins, or other tools is another. It's important to applaud yourself while recognizing the value of letting others know about your accomplishments, as long as you do it gracefully and modestly. To help you identify where you can add more value to your entrepreneur, check out our knowledge tool the "5 Crucial Questions to Make Sure Nothing Falls through the Cracks."[1]

The Law of Perspective

Despite our best attempts to do everything right, we may sometimes approach roadblocks and need to seek the advice and perspective of a respected friend, colleague, or business coach. Acknowledging that you aren't perfect will earn you a great amount of respect in the office.

The Law of Replacing Yourself allows you to feel good about letting go of "how I used to do it," create an opportunity for your future growth, and create a more enhanced future for another team member.

In today's marketplace, we are transforming the employee role; we are creating intrapreneurs in an entrepreneur's world. For the first time, we are able to live in such a way so that everyone wins. It is no longer about climbing the proverbial ladder alone. Imagine your daily life if you started your career with your goal to replace yourself within one year, two years, or maybe five years–it changes the territorial mentality of opportunity. You begin to operate from a position of unlimited opportunity for everyone.

Finally, the fundamental rule when replacing yourself with someone qualified is to make sure you do so in a way that creates a larger future for yourself within the business. It's critical that you do it properly; that means taking the Eight Laws of Replacing Yourself into consideration.

Also, give yourself permission to give up the Law of Perfection. To quote Dan Millman in *The Life You Were Born to Live* on The Law of Perfection,

---

1. Free download at www.yeschick.com

"Practice the simple act of saying 'good enough!' and 'good enough—for now.' Conventionally, nothing and no one is perfect, except flow, change, and fun."

One of the most uncomfortable conversations you will ever have is asking for a raise. It takes courage and confidence to sit down with the boss and initiate a conversation about your pay.

In a small business, employee reviews, annual pay increases, and procedures for promotions are often lacking or nonexistent—and that's a formula for a definitive break in your relationship with your boss that can sometimes become the beginning of the end. It's a perfect storm of misunderstandings, assumptions, disappointments, and missed expectations. You leave feeling underpaid and taken advantage of. How could your boss not give you the raise you want when you work so many extra hours and always have his back? Why should you feel like you have to beg to be paid what you are worth?

Oddly enough, your boss feels exactly the same way. Bosses are often thinking, "How can she ask for a raise when she knows my personal income is down 40 percent and the company is struggling?" How is it possible for two people to leave the same conversation on opposite sides of the fence, but feel the same way? The truth is very simple; people do not discuss salaries, and they likely never will. Your boss has no concept of your struggle because he is struggling as well. When someone is in financial *pain*, he or she does not consider that others might feel that same kind of pain, but on another level or "tax bracket."

The number one reason asking for a raise conjures up such raw feelings is that you and your boss come from two different worlds. Your boss is an entrepreneur, and odds are he hasn't been in the "employee" role in quite a while. You, on the other hand, are fully aware of how awkward and uncomfortable asking for a raise can be. But you may not be aware of some of the pressures your boss faces daily, like bringing in enough new business to pay everyone's salaries and the rising cost of health insurance.

The key to asking for a raise with confidence and in such a way so that you don't feel like you are begging or justifying yourself is to present your proposal to show your present and future value to the company and place a dollar amount on what that value is worth. This is distinctly different from saying, "I work really hard, and it's been a year—can I have a raise, please?" Trust us, if you want the best possible outcome, *you* want to take control of that "raise" conversation.

Don't Ask... Present!

Think about it... if you are asking your boss, the business owner, for a raise, you want to speak his language, right? You want to put it in terms that make sense to him. Well, let's consider how he gets paid. Ultimately, he puts dollars in his pocket from getting clients to hire him. Now, to obtain this money, he doesn't ask clients to hire him... he has to make a presentation of your company's services and conclude it with the price it will cost the client to have these services.

So often we forget that we, as employees, should treat our bosses as we treat our clients. We would never show our worst side to our clients. We make the extra effort to make sure things are presented and prepared well for them. We should do the same for our bosses. Often, when working in a small business, things are casual and you work closely with your boss, which is great, but it can allow us to get too comfortable, or even sloppy, in our presentation to our boss. It's not that you can't be comfortable or even have a friendship with your boss, but you should always make sure you are presenting yourself as a valuable resource. Make sure they have the results you produce–tracking reports, sales numbers, clients billed, and so forth. This is never more important than when you are making a presentation for a raise.

What Your Boss Will Never Tell You about Giving Raises

Do you want to know a big secret? Bosses typically don't know how to give raises, just as you really don't know how to ask for one! They are usually just as uncomfortable having this conversation as you are, and most don't have a set formula or process for calculating what they think is fair, either. Bosses tend to react to your feedback and/or request. You definitely don't want this scenario. Your raise should be based on your value, not on whether your boss had a good or bad day, or how much was in the bank account when you happened to ask for a raise. Also, it should be something the boss can see value in so that he won't regret or rethink it later. There is nothing worse than getting a raise that your boss resents giving.

So, when you feel it's time to discuss a raise, schedule a meeting and prepare a presentation. Never bring personal issues into the conversation (i.e., personal financial struggles, the cost of childcare or tuition, your divorce, etc.) Again, working in a small office can lend an aura of intimacy that sometimes just isn't appropriate in certain conversations, like asking for a raise. It's often hard to draw a line between "what goes" and "what doesn't," but you should be able to tell by instinct and by reading your boss's personality. So, discussing personal issues with your boss depends on your relationship. However, even if you do talk about these things, they don't belong in this discussion about a raise. You should never request or receive a raise based on personal need. You should request and receive a raise based on your value to the company. Use the formula in this chapter to present your value and get your raise.

Getting Started

You'll need to do some homework to get prepared. Set aside 30 minutes and answer the following questions:

1. What is your current annual salary?

2. What is your current bonus system, if any? If you have a bonus system, what is the average amount you make in bonuses per month?

3. What was the date of your last pay raise?

4. What was the amount of the raise then?

5. Since your last raise, what new responsibilities have you taken on? What new skills have you learned? What new roles have you taken on?

6. For each of those, how much money has this brought into the firm or saved for the firm, if you can attach a dollar amount to it.

7. For each item, list how much time it saves your boss.

    (Here's an example. *Since my last raise, I have…*)

    - *Begun drafting trusts, which saves up to two hours per client of your time. We average four clients a month, which equals eight hours, or one day, which is "extra" time for you to now work on other things.*

    - *Begun reviewing all payables before issuing checks for your signature. This reduces your accounting meetings from two hours, twice a month, to 15 minutes, twice a month — saving you 3 and ½ hours of time each month. Additionally, by reviewing payables thus far this year, I've adjusted your cell phone plan to a better one, saving $495 to date. I've also found and have been requesting refunds for various overcharges and incorrect charges, totaling $397. Total savings = $892.*

    Then think ahead and list what you plan on accomplishing over the next year. Most entrepreneurs are forward thinkers, so get them excited about your future goals for the company.

8. List what other roles and tasks you plan to take on, become accountable for, or learn over the next year. Be specific and use the same formula above.

Remember Our Two Rules of Survival from Chapter 1.

1. The company must profit to survive.
2. You must produce value to survive within it.

"It's Not All about Me…But What about Me?"

Now, if you are feeling a little bit like, "Why do I have to list all these facts and numbers? I work hard and it shows," we understand. And fundamentally, your boss probably understands and sees the work you do as well. You even have a good chance that he will give you a raise if you ask for one, even without doing all this proposal work. You don't want a raise if your boss doesn't see the value in it or hasn't thought through it clearly. There is nothing worse than a raise that you feel is being held over your head later or that your boss is resentful of giving.

There's a Time and a Place

Nothing can hijack a conversation more than the wrong time or place. In an already potentially awkward conversation, eliminate distractions and disruptions that can make you lose control of the setting. Carving out quality time to present your proposal is a slippery slope. This doesn't have to be a desperate thing. Don't grab any 10 free minutes your boss might have. That would result in bad timing, lack of his attention, and usually a "let me think about it and get back to you" answer because there isn't enough time to work it through together.

Getting Down to It

So, now you're here for the meeting. Your boss is paying attention, and it's showtime! First, always thank your boss: *"Thank you for taking time out of your schedule to meet with me today. I appreciate it."*

Next, acknowledge him.

"I know you have a lot to do, so I'll keep our time commitment and make sure we stay on track."

Then, get to it.

"I'd like to go over with you where I've grown over the past year and share the value I have produced. I'd also like to talk about where I would like to grow over the next year. I want to make sure it's in line with what you need from me and that you see how I can support you and the firm more. And I'd like to talk about how to value the role I currently play in the firm. I have some ideas I'd like to share with you."

Usually, a boss is more than willing to listen to your suggestions and give feedback, and prefers this to having to come up with all the ideas himself. And usually you end up with a decision closer to what you ultimately wanted if you initiate the ideas!

Now, there's a dangerous pause where you can lose control of the meeting. Let your boss reply, but *don't* let him start throwing out ideas and thoughts. Go over what you have prepared before you start brainstorming about the future.

So, if your boss starts to toss around ideas, politely interject:

"Great, let me jot down what you said so we don't forget that idea, and if I could, let me run through what I've accomplished over the past (time frame since last raise). I found it very interesting when I reviewed it, and I think it will help us see what I am capable of in the future as well."

See how we just "spun" this from being a laundry list of things you have done to an essential part of the "future idea" process? It's much more engaging for a business owner.

Acknowledge the Team

Pay attention to your verbiage so that your presentation doesn't appear as though you are taking credit for everything. For example, if you are calculating the total amount of checks you collected in billing, be sure to always acknowledge your boss and any other team member that played a part in the process.

You don't want the boss thinking, "Hey, she didn't do that all on her own," which is not what you meant. Watch your verbiage and be sure to include "us," "we," "our firm" and not just "I" and "me."

After you have made your presentation, you can say something like:

"These are the things that stood out as most valuable to me. Is there anything else you think I have missed?"

Then transition to the future. This can be tricky, but it doesn't have to be. Typically, we recommend that you don't give your "raise number" yet–just get the boss excited about the future and then drop the number.

So, try something like this:

"So, that sums up what I've learned and accomplished. Thank you for taking time to teach me new things and trusting me to be responsible for new areas. That is a huge compliment for me. I have a suggestion of what I think the value of this role is, but first I'd like to share a few things I think I can also learn and take on over the next year to continue to free you up to work on more important things. And I'd also really like to see where you think I can help. Okay?"

If he pushes for the number now, go ahead and give it. Be confident about it. You've done the research, so be comfortable with the value you produce. But if you can smoothly transition to the future conversation before dropping the number, do it.

Future Conversation

Now, here is another place where you can easily lose control of the meeting. Literally check your watch and allocate *no more* than fifteen minutes to this part of the conversation. The goal of this portion of your presentation is to get a list and/or a general idea of where you and your boss agree and how you can grow in the future. It is not the time or place to get specific about plans of action or details. Get clarity, not a step-by-step plan.

Example:

Boss: *"I'd really like to see you doing initial client meetings. I think you're ready."*

You: *"Just so I am clear on this, you mean replace you doing the initial meetings, with me instead?"*

Boss: *"Yes, I think so."*

You: *"So I would do the presentation, discuss pricing, and get them to hire us, or not? And collect the check? And they would only meet with you after they hired us?"*

Boss: *"Yep. I think with some revision to the presentation, it's something you can do."*

You: *"Okay, I'd love to hear more. I'll schedule another meeting soon for us to talk about which of these ideas we want to act on first. Now, what else do you see?"*

Note how "you" didn't commit to the details. You just agreed that it's an idea that warrants further discussion. If it's something you would love to do, you can even commit to taking that responsibility on, but don't commit to the details of what it looks like until you have a meeting to talk further.

Also, once you present the raise you want end with a closed question, like, "Can you agree to that?" Don't end with an open-ended question like, "What do you think?"

It's Not Fair, It's Your Raise

Always stay away from the word "fair." What is "fair" to one is "reasonable" to another. This is a very subjective word, so refrain from using it. You want your raise based on facts and value. It may put your boss on the defensive if he does counter you or suggest something different, and he will feel the need to justify what his response isn't "unfair." Don't go there because it is a no-win for you and your boss.

If you get anything other than a "Yes," don't shut down. Stay in the conversation and don't give up right away. Remember, your boss is a business owner, many of which are "negotiators". Sometimes they just need to feel they have "tinkered" with a proposal. What changes doesn't have to be the dollar amount. Here are some counter replies:

If your boss counters with a lower amount:

- "I think the results I am producing are valued at the amount I suggested. Is there something that I am doing that perhaps you don't value as much as I do?" This question can help identify things that you do that your boss may not realize are truly valuable. It's good to know these things so you can discuss why they are important or so you can know it's not a priority for you. Focusing on things the boss doesn't think are important won't ever let you move up and make more money.

- "Is there something I could improve upon that would increase my value to the amount I suggested?"

- "Is there something I could take on that would increase my value to the amount I suggested?"

If your boss shares that is it purely a cash flow issue, that he thinks your value is right, but he just doesn't have the cash to pay you, then discuss perhaps having part of your compensation be in the form of bonuses. Set it so that if you help achieve certain cash flow goals, you get paid an extra amount. This way, the money is there to pay for your compensation.

Don't let him say "let me think about it." If you get this reply, ask him directly what other information he needs to make a decision. Try something like this:

- "Do you need more information? Is there a specific part of what I shared that you need to think more about? I want to be accountable for this conversation and not have you take on the burden of solving this. May I help or find what area you are thinking about, or what you are not sure you agree on, so I can consider it also?"

- Often, this will get the boss to tell you what makes him hesitate, and you can solve the question or issue right then.

The Dreaded "Let Me Think about It"

If you get the "let me think about it" response and the above techniques don't work, here are two strategies to try to diminish the crippling effect "let me think about it" has on your forward momentum.

Agree to a specific time frame to come to a decision.

- Okay, how about I schedule 30 minutes next week for us to meet again and make a decision after you have had some more time to think about it?"

- Get a specific time frame to meet again. Do not ever leave it in your boss's head to think about it and get back to you. I promise you, it will not be within the time frame you desire.

- Get an agreement that the raise to which you eventually agree will be retroactive to the date of your meeting. Many times, bosses take months to "think about it," leaving employees with four months of lost increased pay. Always ask if the compensation your boss eventually agrees to can be retroactive to the date you made the request.

  "Okay, I understand you need time to think it over. May I request that once you decide, the compensation be retroactive and effective on today's date? That way, you have time to think it over and neither of us feels pressured to rush into an answer."

Clarify, Verify, and Get Paid

In your excitement about the raise you just nailed, don't forget to secure the details to actually implement your raise! Often, employees thank their boss and run out kicking their heels together with glee and forget to nail down the next steps. Then that great raise that you and your boss are happy about turns into a series of glitches, and everyone gets irritated.

- Clarify the amount and the effective date.

- *You* inform your payroll manager. If your boss is the person who does payroll, offer to email him about it as a reminder.

Avoid Buyer's Remorse

Most bosses just can't help but notice your work habits and performance in the days and weeks directly following a raise. Use this to your advantage. While you have his attention, nail it home that you are worth every penny of what he agreed to pay you.

Don't be a Yes Chick Action Plan: Implement *The Laws of Replacing Yourself*™ and download the following knowledge tools from www.yeschick. com; *How to Ask for a Raise with Confidence*™, *The 5 Crucial Questions to Make Sure Nothing Falls Through the Cracks*™ and *100% Guaranteed Confidence Protectors*

CHAPTER 4

Bitter Chick

How to Not Lose Your Sanity, Your Spirit... and Your Job

"If you had to identify, in one word, the reason why the human race has not achieved, and never will achieve, its full potential, that word would be 'meetings.'"

- Dave Barry, *Things That It Took Me 50 Years to Learn*

Let me share a story with you about an intrapreneur–let's call her Alice. Alice had a job at a wonderful place: a small, fast-paced office with an inventive, creative boss. The days flew by, she was never bored, and the boss was thrilled with her performance. The team respected her and looked to her for answers and advice. She smoothed things out between the team and the boss, helping them both better understand and tolerate each other. She earned the boss's respect by picking up and finishing tasks no one wanted to handle. She was secretly thrilled at how often the boss called her in to share an idea or problem with her to get her insight. The days got a little longer, but that was okay, because she was enjoying her work and knew it would pay off in the end.

One day Alice showed up at her office, Wonderland, Inc., and realized that things were not quite as magical as they once were. Those fun meetings with her boss became long and tedious. He constantly kept her from getting her work done by interrupting her to help him find things or attend an impromptu meeting. The team that used to thank her seemed withdrawn and resistant to her suggestions. Her desk was overflowing with "busywork" because her boss kept giving her tasks that the receptionist usually handled because the receptionist took too long to get it done. Because she was unsure about what was going on, Alice, in her usual take-charge way, knew *she* had to "fix" things.

Over the next few months, Alice began to decline her boss's request for meetings, responsibly explaining that she had a lot of work to complete. She began to ask the team to take their complaints to the boss directly so they could feel more involved with the outcome. She began staying late to get caught up on her work, thinking that if she could just get ahead, things would look better. Alice started to take extra time to type up orders and instructions so she could show the receptionist how to do the tasks. She was also careful to follow up with the receptionist and make sure the tasks were completed so the boss would be pleased.

But as time passed, things didn't improve. Alice's boss began to ignore her suggestions, resentful that she no longer took the time to listen (and agree) to his every idea. The team was indignant that she was "delegating" work to them; after all, she wasn't the "boss." Everyone was frustrated with Alice because they were constantly waiting on her to get something done out of that big pile of work on her desk. She was the bottleneck for everyone.

Her boss wanted to hire a marketing service to help steer the company in a new direction. Alice always used to do that really well, but she was too busy to do that for him these days. He discovered the receptionist had a knack for creating flyers, so he began working with her on new advertisement pieces, which Alice also used to handle.

Worst of all, Alice's day was full of unfinished tasks, unfulfilling work, and constant frustration.

Alice had officially fallen down the rabbit hole! Her boss, who had always been creative and inspiring, now seemed as elusive and hurtful as the Queen of Hearts. The team that used to be friends now seemed to leer at her like Cheshire cats and took the best parts of her job from her bit by bit. Every day was full of dark corners, new characters, and whispered conversations that stopped when she came within earshot.

As an intrapreneur, you play a complicated role on the team. You are an extension of your boss, the entrepreneur, meaning you help make business decisions. You are the team leader, meaning you manage and coach the team. And typically, you are still in a production role, where you have responsibilities of your own, either marketing or work-fulfillment-related. You represent the face of the team to your boss, explaining how the team thinks, sometimes even defending them and fighting for their cause. You also represent the face of the boss to your team, trying to get them to buy into new ideas and the company's direction. Often, it seems each side works against you. While you're in the midst of fighting for the team, they will do something really stupid! In the midst of defending the boss, he will do something to look like the idiot down the hall. Throw in your own heavy workload, and it's enough to make you lose your motivation and decide to go live on a mountaintop in Peru with a llama where there is no cell phone or Wi-Fi service.

As stressful as this is, it is not the worst of it. The true danger is much more insidious. It will sneak up on you amid ringing phones, endless meetings, and piles of work.

Often, as the liaison between the team and the boss, you lose yourself and decrease your value without realizing it. When you strive for a win-win-win outcome but end up with lose-lose-lose, you not only lose the team and the boss, but your own value.

Your mission was to be accessible to your team and to create an honest, reliable, safe place for them to go. At the same time, you are showing value to your boss and trying to maintain your own sanity. Instead, you end up with your boss feeling like you are an overly-paid negotiator constantly bearing gifts of team issues and drama. Your position begins to be a non-cash-flow-producing position, which reduces your value in the boss's eyes. You start to show up like part of the disease vs. the cure.

Have you ever seen the cartoons where Porky the Pig looks at Bugs Bunny and he looks like a big, cooked turkey that makes his mouth salivate? That's you, my friend. You are becoming a turkey! Instead of seeing all your potential, your boss may start seeing the big dollar sign of what he's paying you and begin thinking he can replace you with two new, lower-paid employees who can at least help him get the work off his desk. I'm not saying its fair; it's simply the truth.

At the same time the boss stops seeking your direction for the team, the team stops believing in you. They are not seeing any results from your fight for them. They begin to become "whatever" employees. They are the ones who clock in, clock out, and do just enough to get by, or they begin to go around you and approach the boss directly. As new faces that look willing to work hard and always be "yes" men or women, the boss becomes more receptive to them. They stroke his ego, shake their heads enthusiastically, and tell him how brilliant he is. They are what you were five years earlier.

Meanwhile, your own production is suffering. Even worse, you haven't invested any time into your own personal growth. Others have surpassed you in learning new skills and software. If you are in a marketing role, others have become experts in viral marketing, social media, blogging, and InDesign™ while you were doing busywork to keep the client complaints at bay. If you are in a production role, your production numbers are low because you have been cleaning up messes and catching balls before they drop. Others appear to be able to get things done faster and more accurately than you do. You, my friend, are Alice and have fallen down the rabbit hole where you find that you no longer fit in with your boss or your team. How did this happen? And what do you do?

How Do You Identify the Slippery Slope?

Here are some surefire ways to tell that your job as an intrapreneur with your company is in a precarious position:

- Experts have been hired to do part of your job, and that part hasn't been replaced with something more important.

- You have heard comments or rumors to the tune of, "I can get two like her for the price of one."

- You spend more time answering other people's questions than doing your own work.

- Your boss refers to you as a mediator between him and the team.

- The team looks at you as an extension of the boss because you speak for him.

But Alice Does Get a Paycheck After All…

But hold on. Only through the eye of Alice's looking glass would a job that no longer has the fulfillment and team appreciation it once did feel tolerable when it is actually stunting her growth and happiness. Others will get hired or outsourced while you manage (babysit) the team. And even if you could live with that, the strong foundation of job stability you built erodes each day. You become expendable, like a highly paid cheerleader, and there is little measurable value in that role.

Pulling Alice Out of the Rabbit Hole

We know you have the talent. After all, that's what got you here. You clearly have the drive, determination, and discipline to create a better future, or you wouldn't be reading this book. So let's give you the tools to navigate your way out of the rabbit hole. Let's create a role where your team respects and trusts you and your boss values your position. Let's make sure you feel a sense of accomplishment and fulfillment, and you feel the ability to cultivate future growth.

The Eight Steps to Wonderland

Step 1: Track and share your results.

The absolute number one step to showing the value of your role is by tracking and sharing the results you produce. If you only master one of these steps, this is the most important, because this is your vehicle by which you communicate your value.

First, in order to share your results, you have to track them! Don't fall into the trap of dealing with complicated, time-consuming tracking systems. They bog you down and no one knows how or cares to read the comprehensive reports anyway. Second, figure out what to track! Don't waste time tracking things that your boss doesn't deem important.

1. Write down the three most important things you do in the company.

Think of this from the boss's perspective and consider the things you do that bring money in—either new money or actions to help collect payments. There are innumerable things you can do that are critical to keep the business running, but you can't track everything. And if there isn't cash coming into the company, those other things don't matter anyway.

My Three Most Important Activities	How it Generates Money	Minimum Measurement (what I would have to achieve to keep my job)	Superstar Measurement (what I would have to achieve to make superstar status)
1. Schedule new client appointments .	Brings in potential new clients, which is revenue	Schedule 2 a week	Schedule 5 a week
2.			
3.			

Here are some examples you might list:
a. Book new client appointments.
b. Complete proposals for my boss to use in prospective client meetings.
c. Complete documents for clients' signatures so we can close cases and collect our payments.
d. Send out monthly billing invoices.
e. Schedule speaking events for my boss and market his services.
f. Keep our website updated with new events and products.

2. Review your tracking reports.

Do this with your boss so you can get his input before you go any further. Discuss how to measure your results.

3. Use the Results Tracking Sheet to track your results.

Handwrite it! There is an absolute science in putting pen to paper. Print the worksheet, keep it handy on your desk, and tally your results as they occur. You want this to be quick and easy, not something you revisit at the end of the week and spend two hours completing. And besides, we know you have 10 different things open on your computer screen at any given time, so don't waste time trying to find a spreadsheet each time something happens!

Don't be afraid of measuring your results. Your boss is measuring them, so why shouldn't you? Wouldn't you rather know what you should be shooting for than to be judged unknowingly and possibly unfairly? Your boss will be much more open to helping you reach the goals you set together if you track what you are producing and then discuss what is in the way of you achieving those goals. This attracts your boss's competitive, problem-solving nature.

Set a "minimum measurement"–as in, "What must I produce to earn my paycheck and keep my job?" Again, don't be frightened. It's better that you know this than be surprised one day.

Also set a "superstar measurement." This is the ideal result and your boss would be thrilled if you could achieve it. Plus, this is a great way to have your boss agree to a bonus for achieving "superstar" goals.

4.   Report the results–consistently and quickly!

Decide when you are going to report the results, and do it consistently. If you are going to send a quick e-mail to your boss at the end of each day, listing your results, do it every day and around the same time of day. Then, your boss will begin to expect it, look for it, and appreciate it.

Think of how your boss looks for information naturally. If he sleeps with his beloved Blackberry, then shoot him an e-mail at the end of each day. If he loves to call the office while sitting in traffic and chat with you about his daily schedule, quickly report your results during that call each morning. If he likes the daily schedule printed and placed on his desk each morning, add a short report to it each day. Key word: *short!*

5.   Keep the format consistent.

Don't send an e-mail one day and then print it and leave it on his desk another day.

6.   Report to your team!

a. Remember, don't report to people who don't care. That's annoying and makes it seem as though you're bragging or kissing up. Also, don't just explain the value of what you are reporting to the company, but explain how it impacts them, as well. Include yourself in the example. For instance,

Marketing Faux Pas

It's *extra* important to share these results with your colleagues if your job involves marketing, because the team needs to understand the purpose and the value of this exercise. I can't count the times I've heard, "Oh, she has the fun job, she just plans parties," or "Why is she wasting so much money on brochures and Christmas cards? That comes out of our profit and reduces our bonuses."

So, make sure you report things like these:

- "We have received five referrals from clients after the client appreciation barbecue we did last month. Three went forward, which is $15,000 in new revenue."

- "This year we did two events for client appreciation—a wine tasting and a Christmas card mailing. Our client retention rate is 92 percent, and our renewed business from existing clients this year is $30,000 to date."

- "We have received two referrals from the speaking event our boss did at the new bank last week. I have scheduled two more events for next month."

In our *Relationship Builder Package – Why the Marketing Coordinator Role has Never Produced Results* offers a way to explore how your position adds value to the company and how you can elevate the respect of your team and boss. You can learn more about the *Relationship Builder Package* on our website.

try this:

"Hi, team. I really want to get a big Christmas bonus this year so I can go on vacation, and I know you guys want one, too. So I am going to track how much I send out each month in billing and how much we collect so we have an idea of how the firm is doing profit-wise. This way we'll know whether to expect a good bonus or not. I'll share it with you all briefly in the team meeting, so that if you think of anything else I could do, or anything I miss, let me know because I really want that vacation!"

b. Keep it about "I," what "I" want, and what "I" can do. Show that *you* are making an effort—be the example. Include them in the vision of a great Christmas bonus, but first ask them for help by suggesting that they give you ideas on what to do. Don't give them tasks or suggestions about what *they* can do. They will do this naturally as you start to share your results. Keep it light and make it fun! And make sure the tracking you share is of your own results, not the boss's or theirs!

Step 2: Ask for help with the fun stuff.

The grass is always greener on the other side, right? Sometimes the team may think your job is all fun and hardly any work. And sometimes you *do* get to do fun things, so when that's the case, invite the team to help. Make it productive, not a waste of time. Ask them to bring a potluck lunch so everyone can eat together and then help stuff the gift baskets for a client appreciation dinner. Ask for suggestions for the new Christmas card or narrow down the new logo design to three you like and then ask for a team vote. You can still control the outcome by first narrowing down the possibilities. This also lets the team feel involved and valued. You also never know what hidden talents you have on your team, and you just might be pleasantly surprised!

Step 3: Translate—don't liaison.

Don't become the team's liaison. If you take this route, your boss will see you transform into a cheerleader instead of someone he values for insight. Bosses don't pay cheerleaders. Be the translator—the person who connects the team with the boss, not the person who speaks for them.

As a translator, you need a team member to be there! Stop going in and taking bullets for them because they are too scared to handle things on their own. And stop allowing the boss to discuss issues with you in private. That just makes the team think you are talking behind their backs. Get everyone in the room together, don't take sides, and translate. Taking sides sounds like this: "No, Gloria didn't say she doesn't want to help answer the phones; she said she is behind in her work because she keeps getting interrupted by the phones." Translating sounds like this: "I don't think I heard Gloria say she didn't want to answer the phones; is that what you said, Gloria?" (Note, this requires Gloria to be in the room.) All you did was translate; you straightened out the miscommunication, and now the team member can repeat his/her point.

Or try this: "That isn't what I heard. Gloria, did you say that you don't mind answering the phones?"

Your job as a translator is to ensure that the point of the conversation doesn't get lost in boss-speak and team-speak. You can ensure this by asking questions, not making statements. If Gloria is complaining about answering the phones too much, ask her, "Why are you upset about having to answer the phones?" If her answer is, "That's not my job," you may need to consider the *Smart Fire Solution*™ (found under "Jump Start Coaching" on our website) and see if this is the right team member for your company. If her answer is, "Well, I am getting behind on my work and can't get all the billing out on time," that is important to know!

Don't take sides. Even if you do have an opinion, as a translator it's not your job to sway the outcome. You may get what you want if you take sides, but everyone on the team may not agree with you. Someone is certain to be resentful. If you translate and ask enough questions so everyone sees and understands the issue, then everyone can participate in coming up with a solution that makes them happy.

I like to clarify my role as translator by beginning the meeting with a statement like, "I am here to translate, so if I ask you questions, I am not agreeing with you or questioning you. I am clarifying a point."

Step 4: Don't give the team a fish. Teach them to fish.

Don't take up the team's fight with the boss (which can be hard to do when you think they are right or being treated unfairly). This only puts you back in the cheerleader role in your boss's eyes, and it doesn't teach the team to grow and survive on their own.

Make the team step up and handle things themselves. You can coach them on how to handle a situation and offer to be in the room to "translate" through it, but don't do it for them. The same goes for your boss! If he is having communication problems with a team member, don't offer to handle it for him. Instead, schedule a meeting with both parties and help them through it. It is fine for you, as a team leader, to handle certain issues or conversations with team members but not to handle communication problems.

The best way to do this is by asking questions, not by telling someone the answer or what to do. If your team member is upset at the boss, don't tell her why he was so upset. Instead, ask her, "Why do you think he did that? What would you prefer that he did differently? What do you think you could do to get him to react that way?" Don't think for her, and don't defend the boss. Just facilitate her thought process so that she comes to the conclusions herself and forms her own opinions.

Teaching your team to fish, and to think and act for themselves has innumerous benefits to you and the company. The *Ultimate Smack Down* knowledge tool found on our website is a great way to get your team on the same page, and increase the results and effectiveness of your tasks together. It's just one way you can teach your team to fish.

Step 5: Roll up your sleeves.

I understand that you have to keep an eye on your production. However, you can occasionally roll up your sleeves and get your hands dirty. This commands team respect and loyalty. If the receptionist has a sore throat and is sneezing every five minutes and feels miserable, offer to answer the phones for her so she doesn't have to talk constantly. Or better yet, send her home! If you see the receptionist unloading boxes of supplies, offer to cover the front desk for 15 minutes so she can finish without running up and down the hall to answer the phones at the same time. If you see a team member fighting with the copy machine while your boss is blindly standing there telling her about a case she needs to follow up on, take the copies out of her hands and finish them so she can give her full attention to your boss. You can't do this all the time, or you won't have time to do your own work, but choose your projects wisely and earn your team's respect. You will be surprised that the next time you need someone to stay late at the last minute, your team will volunteer.

Step 6: The D-word.

Never, ever use the word "delegate!" We never liked it, even when we were an entry-level employee. The word implies that the work you ask someone to do isn't exciting. It isn't even about the work itself; it is the method of delivery. The boss moved a team member named Christina into an assistant role and told her that Laney was really busy and needed to delegate work to someone he could trust. He thought he was complimenting her by showing that the company trusted her enough to promote her. And for a few days, that worked. But quickly, items "delegated" by Laney to Christina began to show up like "dirty work" to Christina. Think about it, when you delegate something you are basically saying, "I am really busy and important, and my skills are better used elsewhere, so here, you can do this. This is more your speed." That's not very empowering. Now, had Christina been promoted to a project manager role, rather than assistant, and understood the importance of the project and its potential revenue to the company, she could have taken on her tasks with a sense of purpose and empowerment and may have exceeded everyone's expectations.

Don't ever delegate. Ask people to support you, work with you, and apply their fantastic skills to something. Basically, you need to "sell" the work to them, not delegate it to them. It might take extra time, but it takes far less time than having to handle employee attitude problems or having to fire and rehire team members and finish the project yourself in the process. A great term to use instead of the word delegate is, "I'd like to train you on being accountable for X. I've been impressed with your work and think you are ready for more responsibility."

Step 7: Always, always lead by example.

This is such a cliché that it's overlooked in every company we've worked with. It's fundamentally simple: If you are late to meetings, your team will be late. If you gossip, your team will as well. If you don't complete projects on time, neither will they. If you don't come to meetings prepared, don't be surprised when your boss schedules over them. You never say, "Oh, to hell with it, I'll just show up unprepared." You have very valid reasons why this occurred. But remember whenever you encounter team habits you don't like, you may have given permission for them to occur. You may have inadvertently left the impression that the team has a valid reason for being late and unprepared.

Step 8: Don't break trust.

Time and again, we see teams and bosses break trust with a co-worker out of the best intentions. We aren't talking about gossip; we're talking about sharing private information with the best of intentions. For example, if the boss is ranting about his assistant's poor performance and you know she is having marital problems, and you allude to that so the boss won't misjudge her. You just broke trust. So, you can say, "That's odd; isn't your assistant typically very dependable?" When he says yes, suggest he take her to lunch and provide a safe place for her to share her experiences if she feels so inclined. Or you can say, "Usually when a great employee suddenly has performance issues, something might be wrong that we need to know about."

Or, you can approach the employee and say something like, "Do you think your marital problems are impacting your job at all? Do you think you should at least tell the boss you are having some personal problems so he doesn't think you are slacking off?"

So, how are you feeling now? Did this exercise leave you feeling enlightened and re-energized? Or do you feel like saying, "Yeah, that was great, but nothing in my core has changed. I am not feeling the excitement and possibilities of a fertile ground for cultivation of future growth." Now what?

As we write this, we are living in one of the worst economic times of our generation's history. You may often find yourself "justifying" why "good enough" has become acceptable. You hear this remark from no fewer than five people a day: "Just be grateful you *have* a job." You look around your communities of friends, family, and neighbors and hear people complaining about their jobs. You are seeing layoffs hit closer and closer to your circles every day. Family members are told they have to take a 40 percent salary cut to remain employed in a world with a national unemployment average of 8.5 percent.

Giving up Control for Growth

Intrapreneurs struggle with giving up the control of handling all team/boss relations. Many of these steps teach the boss and team to interact with each other with a little coaching and translation so that you can fade into the background. This can be scary to a person who has been instrumental in keeping the company running. Get out of the rabbit hole, Alice! If the team and boss can interact with a minimum of your time and energy, you can master your own job and produce amazing results!

And you know that your plugging away at 10 percent is better than most at 100 percent. You feel a bit of comfort in this, but then you begin to notice you're sad all the time, experiencing insomnia for the first time in your life, waking up at 2 a.m., not exercising, and having that horrible "nervous stomach" feeling all the time. Anger and resentment have become your daily companions. You now understand what it means to feel depressed, empty, and lost. These emotions are hitting a little too close to home these days. On top of all that, you feel as though there is nowhere on this planet where you belong. What do you do?

Do not fret. Take what comfort you can in knowing that you are most absolutely not alone. Feel comfort in the work that you have done and have confidence that you did the best work you could to get to this place. You have found yourself at the starting point of the Intrapreneur Movement™. Keep reading! Help is on the way!

Don't be a Yes Chick Action Plan: Identify the slippery slopes on page 76, track and share your results, download the knowledge tool *The 5 Crucial Questions to Make Sure Nothing Falls through the Cracks* ™.

CHAPTER 5

Yes Chick

Why You Don't Want to be One

*"Whenever you find yourself on the side of the majority,
it's time to pause and reflect."*

- Mark Twain

The tiny ship was tossed... if not for the courage of the fearless crew the minnow would be lost... the minnow would be... FOCUS! I shake my head and tune into my boss's monologue on the company's "new" (as opposed to last quarter's "breakthrough") marketing direction. For the last 45 minutes, he has waxed nostalgic, rehashing the same ideas we've discussed for the past eight months. The theme song from "Gilligan's Island" keeps sneaking into my head and I struggle to stay with the conversation—well, the monologue. My boss excitedly starts waving his hands, and people nod. My boss "explains" louder, people nod more. *...the minnow would be lost... the minnow...* STOP! PAY ATTENTION! He's asking me a question. Uh-oh, it's not a rhetorical one!

"What do you think?" the boss asks.

Heads nod eagerly. Murmurs of "great," "love it," and "oh, absolutely" blend with the shuffling sounds of notebooks closing and materials being gathered. The team begins moving around to get up and leave.

Is it the moment of truth?

No, you know the truth. This plan has some flaws. And I won't even ask if you think you should speak up, because you know you should. What does truth have to do with speaking up or keeping quiet?

Wait! It's the moment of *trust*.

Do you trust your boss to be receptive to an honest critique of his ideas? Does he respect that you want what is best for the company even if it means disagreeing with him?

Do you trust your team to listen and give you their honest feedback? Or will they nod their heads and agree just to get out of the meeting as quickly as possible, but then spend the next 20 minutes bitching at the water cooler about what a waste of time it all was and how they zoned out and went to their "happy place."

Most importantly, do you trust yourself? Do you trust that maybe you *do* see something wrong with the plan that others don't? Do you trust that everyone isn't just smarter than you are and that your comments will be ridiculed? Or, better yet, that you will be fired?

This is your defining moment. Will you be a "Yes Chick" or make the transformation to become an intrapreneur?

What is a Yes Chick?

Let's be true to ourselves—we all know what a Yes Chick is. We've all been next to one in meetings or been annoyed by them at times, yet most of us steadfastly refuse to consider that we might actually *be* a Yes Chick.

I mean, sure, we let a few bad ideas slide by without commenting, but after all, the boss didn't really ask anyone for opinions, and who am I to jump in, anyway? What do I know? I've never owned or run my own business.

And sure, it was irritating when no one on the team attended the marketing meeting with last week's action plan and progress reports on what they completed and what is still pending. That entire two-hour meeting was a total waste of time. But who I am to question the team and hold them accountable? Plus, we created an entirely new plan because we weren't prepared, so the boss took the reins and did his "quick start" thing.

If these sound like familiar phrases, you might be sliding into Yes Chick territory. Let's take a look at why you, an independent, confident professional, would be letting your moments of truth pass you by, and see what you can do about it!

A Yes Chick is someone who nods her head and agrees even when she really has a better suggestion or approach that could save time, money, and frustration. A Yes Chick hears an idea that will cost the company money and manpower, but goes with the general consensus rather than objecting. A Yes Chick gets annoyed when others don't complete projects and tasks on time, but she doesn't speak up and object to it.

A Yes Chick isn't hard to define. And it's not a matter of being a "coward." It is how we've been conditioned, or programmed to "do a good job" and keep our mouths shut. What's hard to reconcile is how on earth you got to be here, and now that you are, what to do about it.

Molly remembers the defining moment of truth when she realized she was slipping into the Yes Chick zone:

> *We had hired a marketing company that we paid a big (no, huge) monthly retainer for 12 months to take the company to the next level. Being in a small company of three and serving as the CEO/Marketing Department/Billing Department, you get the*

idea. I was naturally responsible for managing the marketing company. We hired them for their reputation in the marketplace and for their track record of taking like-minded organizations to the next level. My role was to manage, direct, and lead them in the company's new direction and meet deadlines and so forth.

Month Two:

The president of the marketing company called me and said, "We can't work with him. He is a steamroller, and my team won't get on another marketing call with him— he's all over the map. His ego is out of control and he won't listen. We prefer to only deal with you because you get the job done and you're a focused pit bull. We love it."

Month Seven:

After spending a tremendous amount of time on a major website project, the boss decides the work we've done is worthless and we need to go in a different direction. Note: The "boss" never had time to look at the website and "delegated" (visit our website for "STOP using THE 'D' Word" tool book, or refer back to Section 6 in Chapter 4) the entire project to me because he "trusted" me.

During a weekly marketing meeting, back when I was a Yes Chick and let him run (destroy) the agenda, he decided that we were going to "talk website" because the buddy he had breakfast with told him the five "musts" of every website, and five minutes before our call he pulled it up and wanted to change (trash) seven months of work. Then the boss said it: "So this project was priority number one. In fact, drop everything we are working on and let's hop on a plane and get Molly and me in a room for two days with the web team and implement this powerful stuff. If we don't, no client will ever hire us. We're dead in the water."

We were all deflated, but hell, we could do it. If he is this passionate about the website and what he has learned, even though he is paying a national marketing company that has NASCAR as a client, we're in. My friends can keep my two kids so as to not interrupt my hubby's work schedule too much. I'm in; I'll get on the plane.

The marketing firm prepared for our arrival and put three full-time employees in a conference room with us for two days. Everyone was ready to put this project that we had worked on for so long and hard to bed. Two days, slam dunk—it will be done!

Day One:

We met with the web team and its graphic designers. The boss began the meeting with a brief "history" of the company. He took them through three hours of technical-legal mumbo jumbo that clearly neither one of them understood (or cared about). Their eyes glazed over and they nodded their heads, saying, "Wow that is interesting." Then he went on and on about vision, mission, and standards-never once going through the website page by page.

We walked out with our heads spinning. We had no clear direction. It had been a complete waste of time.

Day Two:

The web team didn't even show up. He had annoyed them so much that the owner of the company asked them to not even go in because it would be another day of the same thing. So, here we are, the boss and me, in a city away from office and home, sitting there alone. The boss and I started talking numbers, recreating an annual budget and bonus structure that we have created two times before but still hadn't implemented. We then moved to the "future direction of the company" conversation; you know, that one that entrepreneurs like to have when they want to get out of actually doing the task at hand.

At 9 a.m., I realized I had to catch my plane in five hours. At that point, I said to myself, "I will sit here and nod, then quit when I get home." Then I had an epiphany. I realized that I was just as responsible for this conversation and the direction of my future as he was. Seriously, I had heard people speak of those "light bulbs" going off, but I'd never gotten it. But I got it then.

Immediately, I stopped him dead in his tracks and requested a time-out. In that moment, I chose to abandon Plan A—an unprofessional hissy fit that would include two or three "F bombs" and a bucketful of tears. That would be the "old," non-confrontational Molly in rare form. Instead, I chose to dig deeper into my toolbox. I announced, "We need to stop and talk about what is not working, not only in this conversation, but for me in my professional role."

What came out of that conversation changed my life without question. We had an honest, respectful discussion that fused our adult, professional relationship closer, and I won a deep respect from my boss because of who I chose to be in that moment. He also appreciated that I would help him see his blind spots and not allow him to show up in disarray or not hold him accountable. Since that day, December 8, 2009, we have worked very skillfully together. What came out of our meeting became known as our House Rules of Engagement.

House Rules of Engagement

As a team, we agree to use the following House Rules of Engagement every day to allow us to grow and eliminate any unnecessary dividedness:

- *Refrain from "holding on to stuff," ask and expect honesty while maintaining respect;*
- *Send The Daily Dish™ at the end of each day to keep the team informed, not to micromanage;*
- *Walk into every situation and meeting with Facts Without Emotions™;*
- *Attend every Meeting and Team Huddle:*
- *Schedule our appointments and meetings with a clear intent;*
- *Declare our purpose and intended result;*
- *End with specifics attached to implementation;*
- *Every person has absolute permission to hold each other accountable and must be accountable for his or her own actions;*
- *Speak respectfully to one another;*
- *EVERYTHING is ALWAYS "on the table" with a "CAN-DO" approach;*
- *We agree to always engage in Healthy Conflict to solve real problems quickly and to put critical topics on the table for discussion;*
- *We agree as a team to always be willing to FAIL FORWARD (concept from the book by John Maxwell).*

These are the two most important lessons I learned that day:

1. *The determining factor for your happiness with your job is your level of courage to have the honest, while respectful, conversations. You can take responsibility for what is occurring around you and stop placing blame, as blame is merely a hideout for not facing what is not working in your life.*

2. *Not only did my relationship with my boss change for the better, but I approached my work with a sense of ownership and leadership that moved my confidence meter up 10 notches. We walked out of that meeting with immediate Rules of Engagement, and I knew I had to hold up my end of the bargain. My boss was committed to follow through by giving the business to me and putting all his trust in me, so it was time to take my game up a notch. And that is something I will take with me and grow with every day my feet hit the floor, no matter where I am going.*

Yes–the Right Answer for the Wrong Job

Yes-ing the boss, even for the best reasons, is a temporary reprieve from dealing with reality. It might be the right answer for the moment, but it's the right answer for the wrong job. Yes-ing the boss will redefine you and your job into a most undesirable role.

Yes–The Temporary Ego Booster

Yes-ing the boss can be seductive. After all, when you start agreeing and stop questioning, you become a very attractive sounding board. Entrepreneurs are business owners, who, by nature, stick their necks out for potential attack more than others–their confidence is constantly challenged. Their clients question their pricing and value, their competitors pick them apart, their team questions them, and they are always out on a limb, taking chances and forging into the unknown. It can be easy for you to slip into the Yes Chick role. You nod and lie low to preserve your confidence and sanity. Your boss keeps coming to you for an easy nod of approval because it feels good for someone to finally not question or debate him.

Your Moment of Truth

For those of you still in denial, here are The Five Truths that identify you as a Yes Chick:

1. You nod your head in agreement to a mediocre idea because you are starving or because everyone else is nodding as well.

2. You knew your boss's statement was incorrect, but out of pure frustration due to him overruling the agenda and taking over the meeting, you keep quiet rather than spend a tortuous hour tiptoeing around his ego and correcting him.

3. You suffer through a wasteful meeting going over information because your boss has other business ventures and doesn't remember what he discussed in your last meeting, and/or team members were supposed to have prepared before the meeting rather than rescheduling it when they *are* prepared.

4. You don't understand a shared idea or concept, but the little voice in your head told you to keep quiet because everyone else there was more qualified than you, and after all, they "got it."

5. You've been cornered in the kitchen by a team member complaining about the boss and even though you think the boss was right, you nod and sip coffee until you could make an escape.

This dream world of yeses, however, is a fragile and temporary one. Small businesses are quick to shatter fantasies, and the bottom line will always tell the truth, even if you don't. Soon, bad ideas and faulty plans will reveal themselves.

When ideas bear no fruit, your boss's ideas become "our" ideas that didn't work. And frankly, if you nodded your head and agreed, he would be right on that one! You don't help the business by letting your boss spend time, money, and resources on bad ideas.

Worker Bee Syndrome

A constant yes-er can also yes herself right into the Worker Bee Syndrome. Every true entrepreneur will eventually tire of someone who constantly agrees with him because there is no challenge. Questioning an idea forces an entrepreneur to "sell it" to you, and every entrepreneur loves to sell his ideas. A good debate forces an entrepreneur to brainstorm and think an idea through. Selling their ideas is a mental Disney World for entrepreneurs; being faced with a Yes Chick leaves very little on the mental playground to intrigue him.

> *"The highest compliment my boss ever paid me was when he said 'I love sharing my ideas with Laney because she questions them, which forces me to think through the possible pitfalls. I know if I can sell her on it, I can sell anyone so I'm more than confident and prepared to take an idea to a client."* – Laney Lyons

Once the ego-boosting of constant yes-ingis is over, most entrepreneurs will lose interest in sharing ideas with a Yes Chick. They'll also lose some respect for Yes Chicks. They may still like you, but because they are risk-takers, they will always have the highest level of respect for those who take chances, are willing to put themselves out there to share an idea or thought, and ultimately tell the truth.

By being a Yes Chick, you will relegate yourself to being a Worker Bee as well. In your entrepreneur's eyes, your opinion becomes less valuable because it isn't authentic. It really has no value because he is getting nothing from your opinion that he doesn't already have. Your opinion or lack thereof mirrors his own, so he won't need you anymore. The only other reason he might keep you on the payroll is if he can put you in a Worker Bee role.

By becoming a Worker Bee in your boss's eyes, you immediately become expendable and replaceable. Work production can be replaced, but your thinking cannot. Your thoughts make you unique; completing work, no matter how much and how fast you can do it, does not.

If business slows down and revenue must be cut, a Worker Bee is the first to be eliminated. A thinker, however; is needed to help solve business problems and will find their job more secure.

Our Definition of Worker Bee

One who is viewed by the boss as only good for producing work, moving papers, and completing tasks. While recognized as valuable, a Worker Bee is replaceable by another person who can complete tasks, move paper, and produce work. Often, a Worker Bee is replaced by technology or a cheaper model that can do the work faster.

Masters in Business–For FREE

Most importantly, by being a Yes Chick, you miss the opportunity to grow and learn. By working in a small business, you get a real-life business degree, for free! In fact, you get paid for it, but you have to recognize it and reach out and take it. By being truthful and asking tough questions, you get to take part in discussions about everything from marketing to infrastructure to budgets and profits. By being a Yes Chick, you miss the opportunity to take part in this education and growth. It's a safe route, at least temporarily, but one with few rewards.

The Ultimate Dysfunction–Lack of Trust

The book, *The Five Dysfunctions of a Team: A Leadership Fable* by Patrick Lencioni, identifies what we believe is the ultimate dysfunction in any relationship–lack of trust. In a relationship, if you feel like you can't be honest in your disagreement about an idea or plan, you lack trust. Either you don't trust yourself or you don't trust your boss. Debate is healthy; lack of trust creates a broken foundation, upon which no solid growth can be built.

Empowered Role

If you are ready to create a role in which your opinion may not always be the most popular, but will always be respected, stop the yes-ing and start taking responsibility for your voice and your cause in the matter. You will be amazed at how empowering and authentic it will feel for you. And the strategic byproduct is that you will start to notice that people stop coming to you with complaints and drama, but for honest coaching and feedback instead.

Use the techniques in this chapter to learn how to speak up in a way that will make people listen.

And remember, your boss doesn't pay you to shuffle papers; he pays you to ask him the questions that no one else will. You are a pioneer, embrace it.

Don't be a Yes Chick Action Plan: Follow the Rules of Engagement, recognize when you are being a Yes Chick, and check out the knowledge tool *How to Eliminate Useless Meetings* ™, available at www.yeschick.com.

CHAPTER 6

Smart Chick

Controlling Your Workplace, Not Letting it Control You

"The speed of the boss is the speed of the team."

- Lee Iacocca

Keeping Your Boss Focused

It's 8:00 a.m. You are checking your voicemail, half-listening, as the receptionist hovers over you, asking you how to answer a client's question. In your ear, a slightly miffed client is on your voicemail asking where the "stuff" is that your boss said he would send three weeks ago. Your cell phone rings, displaying your boss's number. He tells you he will be in the office shortly and needs to meet with you to go over a few things from his appointments the day before. You freeze, knowing you had set aside this morning to prepare documents for his noon appointment. As you tune back in, your boss is waiting on the phone for your reply, your receptionist is looking at you for a response to her question, and your voicemail drones on.

Do you find most of your days end up like this no matter how hard you work to create your ideal day?

It's frustrating to lose control of your day, but you can either throw your hands up and decide to "do the best you can" or take charge, set limits, and refuse to let your day—and your team—push you around.

But that's not always realistic. How can you keep your boss focused on his job when you can't get anything done yourself because you spend your day running around behind him trying to follow up with clients he forgot to call, send emails he didn't answer, and clean up his mess? And when you *do* get a moment to try to get some work done, he asks you to meet with him for an impromptu meeting, for which you aren't prepared. But how do you explain this to your boss, whom you respect and, who, after all, signs your paycheck?

Well, we really suggest that you *not* try to explain to your boss all the things he does that drive you crazy. After all, he isn't trying to drive you crazy on purpose. If he knew how to be more organized and effective, he would. But he's not, and that's why he hired you. So take a deep breath and start over!

Why is This Your Problem?

Depending on how tired you are, you may be asking yourself varying degrees of the question, "Why is this my problem?" After all, you work hard, you do the best you can, and there is only so much you can do. But it *is* your problem. You are constantly interrupted with "got a minute?" You never feel prepared. You spend more time chasing your tail than getting your work done.

Don't Be a YES CHICK!

Fortunately, for the overworked, exhausted intrapreneur, solving this problem doesn't require you to work harder. It requires you to work smarter.

With some simple techniques and strategies, you can coax your boss to move in the right direction and save your sanity in the process.

Working harder won't solve the fundamental problem. It will only leave you more exhausted and strained. Solving the problem requires directing the boss's focus to the most important issues (read: revenue-producing priorities) of the day.

Is Your System Broken?

In case of a system breakdown (or a nonexistent one), check out these identifiers to determine whether you need to build or repair your system:

- You are having too many meetings that garner no measurable results.

- Your boss is constantly catching you off-guard, asking for things for which you aren't prepared to answer.

- You're being called to mandatory company "meetings" more and more often throughout the week.

- You are constantly catching your boss off-guard with questions and things you need from him.

- You often find your boss doing something other than what he agreed to work on during that specific time.

- You see a pattern of the company switching business models and/or directions in an effort to bring in additional revenue.

> The techniques below can help you solve the disorganization of time and information between an entrepreneur and an intrapreneur. However, it won't fix the fundamental problem of integrity. If you and/or your boss are not operating with integrity and the ability to be honest with each other, no technique will fix the inevitable consequences. If you and/or your boss are not working within your Unique Ability and have no passion for what you do, no technique in the world will work.

Working Smarter

However, there's good news. Typically, the trouble is that the entrepreneur

- 94 -

is really only suffering from a lack of focus. It comes with the territory. The following *Boss Focus Techniques: Nine Ways to Respectfully Direct Your Boss*™ are effective keys to support you on a daily basis and boost everyone's productivity.

1. Schedule Twice-Weekly Marketing Huddles

Wait, don't close the book. I know you think this is a sneaky way to trick you into a "meeting." We are all sick and tired of meetings, but hear us out. A purposeful huddle during which you move projects forward and make decisions is a good thing. It's just the never-ending meetings where nothing gets resolved that drive us intrapreneurs crazy. Use this Marketing Huddle as a defensive technique. When your boss asks you to talk to him about marketing-centered ideas, write down the discussion point or idea on the Marketing Huddle agenda and remind him that there is a scheduled time to discuss marketing. This sounds like "Great! I'll put that on the list to go over in our Marketing Huddle tomorrow morning!" When you come across something marketing-related that you need to discuss with your boss, hold it for your huddle. This designated time becomes the time and place for marketing discussions, which keeps everyday interruptions to a minimum. (If you have too many meetings that are preventing you from getting your job done, take a look at the knowledge tool on our website *How to Eliminate Useless Meetings.*)

2. Set Boundaries

Set boundaries and stick to them. Be clear about what you will and won't do. For example, when you are in the middle of your Marketing Huddle and your boss starts checking e-mail or Googling a topic you are discussing, remind him that he wanted you to be productive and that you could use those 10 minutes to get the work done for him. When he opens a browser, politely get up, leave the meeting, and go back to work. Do not go outside the boundaries of your Marketing Huddle agenda. He hired you because he needed your direction, so give him that direction, and give him just a little while to adjust. He'll get it.

3. Permission Standards

Permission standards help you define standard answers for the most common problems that can generally block the workflow. They allow you to immediately solve a problem or answer a question without having to ask your boss for a decision, which can cause a slowdown. For example, it's common to go to your boss when a client asks for a discount. But this either takes too long to get an answer, causing you to lose the client, or it invites a complete re-discussion about pricing, which wasn't the issue. And nine times out of 10, you lose the client in the meantime anyway. If you don't want to constantly ask for permission, create standards (rules) within which you have permission to operate without checking with your boss. Perhaps you can agree that you are allowed to offer up to a 10 percent discount without having to check with your boss. This allows for quicker response to potential clients and avoids the potential pitfall of constantly recreating your pricing. Or perhaps you have to check with your boss on whom to refer people to for different types of services. Instead, create a list of approved professionals to recommend so you can use it without having to check with your boss every time this situation occurs. For two weeks, keep a list of questions to ask your boss. Then choose the most common ones and create standards around them. This will make you and the company look competent, be more efficient and save a lot ot time.

4. Radical Change

By this, we mean starting with the biggies-take away your boss's voicemail and e-mail. WHAT? Calm down. We understand this does look like more work for you to have your boss's e-mails and voicemails routing to you. But think about the amount of time you spend tracking things down and the clients who get irritated while waiting for your boss to respond to them. If you can be the point of contact, you can route calls accordingly. Many times clients don't even need to talk to your boss. Someone else can assist the client in his place. Also, this way, you will always know what is going on and won't be caught off-guard with requests. Rather than your boss exchanging a series of e-mails with a client and promising them something he can't fit into his schedule, you can talk to the client, clarify the project, and schedule a meeting or appropriate next action that fits into everyone's schedule. You will also find a lot of free stuff and time your boss is giving away to clients. This strategy can actually increase revenue by you making sure client's are aware of the charge for certain things they are requesting and that they are billed for it. The few extra minutes you spend handling the client's call is FAR less than the amount of time you spend currently fixing the mess!

5. Make it Fun and Funny

Humor is a great way to handle potentially awkward or tense situations. A fun way to approach your boss when he gets off track is to play the "Show Me the Money" game. Make a game out of keeping him focused. Use play money, and each time you catch your boss goofing off, make him give you one dollar of play money. But it works both ways, too. Each time you interrupt him when he is working on a task to which you both agreed, you have to give him one dollar back. At the end of the week, cash the play money out for real money, or use it as credit towards time off, a Starbucks gift card, or whatever you want. It's a fun way to ease the tension of holding each other accountable. It's much less offensive to yell, "You owe me a buck!" than "Why aren't you doing what you are supposed to do, like you said you would?"

6. Growth Days

Schedule days to work on the growth of the firm. We call these Growth Days. They are different from Money Days, which are days when your boss meets with clients or gives presentations, or whatever brings in money. They are different from Construction Days, also, which are days when your boss "works on getting work done," such as preparing documents, completing paperwork, and so forth. Growth Days are when the firm gets together to specifically work on projects that will grow the business. It's good to create scheduled time to work on these things so they don't interrupt tasks that bring in money and work that must be completed. Usually your boss is excited about these growth projects, so he may be apt to want to work on these things. However, there are some keys to having a productive Growth Day:

- *Chip away at the BIG elephant, one small step at a time.* Schedule four hours each Friday afternoon, during which the whole company can work together on a Growth Project.
- *Start with lunch, in house, on the company.* The rest of the day is 100% Growth Day.
- *Do only ONE project at a time.*
- *Don't move to another project until you finish the first one, especially when you are almost at the finish line.*
- *Don't cancel or reschedule. Keep it going. If someone misses out, they miss out.*
- *Report your progress every Monday in your weekly team meeting and create a game plan for your next Friday growth day (visit our website for a FREE Growth Day Focuser, www.yeschick.com).*
- *Each project should ONLY have a 90-day shelf life. No more. If it's a really big project, break it down into smaller 90-day projects to accomplish.*
- *Celebrate it!* Celebrate your success! Bring in donuts and congratulate the team for completing a project. Energy is contagious! (And it feeds off donuts.)

7. Construction Days

Just as your company needs Growth Days, it also needs Construction Days. Blocking a few hours each week to tackle large work-related projects helps both you and your boss stay up to date on the larger scope of things. When you schedule production time, be sure to have an agreed to-do list to tackle. If not, you and your boss will show up with different ideas of what you need to do.

8. Money Days

And just as your company needs Growth Days and Production Time/ Days, it also needs Money Days. I like to schedule Money Meetings each week. These are appointments where your boss meets with clients, referral sources, and so on. I never like to put off Money!

9. Less is More

Don't take on too much. Remind your boss if you and the team are overwhelmed and overworked. Is it because you're not working efficiently and wasting time (be honest)? Do you need to schedule a time to analyze if it's simply because you have too much work and need to figure out what you can do about it? All the time management tips in the world won't give you more than 24 hours in a day and seven days in a week. It's more about what you intentionally focus on during the time that you have. When your boss is offered a fun new project to be a part of, when a fellow colleague asks for a "huge" favor, or when they're thinking about volunteering... stop and hold them accountable to their priorities. The next time he is invited to speak at a Rotary Meeting that hasn't produced one stitch of work in the 10 years that he has been "networking" with, maybe it's time your remind him. Remember, if your day is already full and if you take on new work, "something's gotta give" and something always will not get done. It's your choice to prioritize and decide what will be at the top of the list.

One small change that has helped us tremendously is the knowledge tool "Tips for Weekly Effectiveness," a free download at www.yeschick.com. There's nothing more productive than setting up your week to start off on the right foot, and getting everyone on board as well.

Research consistently exposes that most employees quit because of a damaged relationship with their boss or manager. Intrapreneurs and employees across the board simply do NOT quit jobs--they quit bosses. Most new managers move into their roles because they have a Unique Ability in their industry and they have proven it over the years. They rarely begin their management careers with the experience, training, and support they need to effectively manage others.

It's amazing how many times we are coaching a company where the boss and the key team members are struggling and operating sideways. Then, when everything's out on the table, we discover that both are trying to accomplish the same exact thing–get work done, money in the door, and grow the company all while practicing work/life balance. The team and boss just can't work in sync, which leads to mutual frustration. This is a very dangerous situation. It can go from moderate irritation to deep-rooted resentment of each other that is hard to repair. Many great teams have been broken because this has been ignored. The devastating part is you are both striving for the same goal. Everyone is working hard. And with the few, easy to implement techniques shared in this chapter you can get back on the same page, move the minutia out of the way, and grow the business.

How to Lead Your Boss

Have you ever worked with a boss who spoke a mystery language? Little catch phrases that he used on a daily basis to try to convey some very important point to you and each time that phrase was uttered with passion and determination you shook your head and walked away in confusion? Sayings like "I need you to step up," "I need someone to take the ball and run with it," "be accountable," "think…" Those sayings sound great, and you even find yourself agreeing with them. Then you go refill your coffee, sit at your desk ready to "step up" and "run with the ball" and… wait a minute, what are you actually supposed to DO to step up? Run with *what* ball? What do these mystery words that your boss utters with such desperation and conviction really mean in your day-to-day work life?

Your boss may not specifically ask you or say that he wants your assistance or help, but in reality he is begging for it. Each time he asks you to "step up" he is asking you to help him. Often he isn't clear about WHAT specifically he wants you to do, because he himself doesn't even know! Really, he doesn't. He can go on and on in a motivating speech about opportunities for you and being all that you can be, but truth be told, he doesn't always specifically know what day-to-day tasks you can do to help him. So, we'll share the secret with you. There is no specific day-to-day task that will allow you to step up or run with the ball, because its not a "to do" item, it's a change of mindset. He doesn't want you to simply come in with a notepad and leave with a "to do" list of his instructions to follow. HE WANTS YOU TO HELP HIM LEAD! In fact, he is begging you to.

Now you might be asking yourself why your boss, brilliant entrepreneur that he or she is, wants you to help him or her lead. It's really quite simple but very exhausting to be the sole decision-maker. Think about your entrepreneur.

Yes, entrepreneurs are "Unique Creatures." As innovators and risk-takers, they are often at a loss for people to talk to who really understand what they are trying to accomplish. They are usually up to "bigger things" than others in their family or social circle. They are viewed as "wacky," "absent-minded professors," "brilliant but a little off" and people are constantly coming to them for solutions to problems, for motivation, and for encouragement. But to whom does the entrepreneur turn for solutions, motivation, and encouragement? His spouse may or may not be familiar with the inner workings of his business, so she is probably not a good sounding board for your entrepreneur. On top of that, many spouses have a "leave work at work" rule. Aside from his spouse, with whom does your entrepreneur spend most of his time? His employees—you! Now look at all the people who your entrepreneur spends most of his day with and count how many of them depend on him for answers, advice, money, direction, leadership and encouragement? So at the same time that they are viewed as "wacky," many people depend on their boss. Now do you understand why they may need help leading?

Leaders today aren't just bosses; they're self-starters who take charge even when they haven't been given the authority. They absolutely squash the "it's not my job" mantra that so many employees make a truth every day.

If you are reading this book, you probably aren't the normal "it's not my job"-type employee. However, you might unconsciously be the "that's someone else's job"–type employee. Both types may sound the same, but there's a big difference. The "it's not my job" people don't care if the task gets done. The "it's someone else's job" people just assume someone else will handle it, so it doesn't occur to them to step in and handle it themselves. Their intentions aren't bad; they care, but they have blinders on and only see their day-to-day tasks laid out in front of them.

Leaders, on the other hand, are their boss's eyes and ears. They take off the blinders and accept that the entire business is their responsibility. They may not know how to do every task, but they will step in and make sure someone is handling things; they don't just assume it's handled. Most importantly, leaders not only have their entrepreneurs' backs, *but they equally have their fronts as well.*

Leading refers to an *intentional* practice of working with your boss to obtain the best results for you, for him, and for the company. It's getting your boss to be invested in your success by noticing you as a key player, not by showing off your excellence in your respective job area but by doing what's best for the business. Leading means being a team leader–stepping in and being that force that redirects a team when they have fallen off-course. It's being the first one to roll up their sleeves and get to work. It's being the one to have a positive

Having Your Boss's Backs, AND their Fronts

What does this mean? You are probably familiar with having someone's back. You know, making sure things get done, following through, not leaving a task undone, and making sure all bases are covered. But in this attempt to always have your boss's back, many employees overlook having their boss's front. Think of your boss as being an actor on a stage. Indeed, they are. They are onstage with clients, potential clients, referral sources, money sources and even with their team. They are selling, inspiring, leading, and earning people's confidence in them. Having a boss's front means doing what it takes to make sure they look good onstage, no matter what. It goes beyond making sure the lights and stage props are in the right place.

You could pleasantly tell a client that your boss is stuck in traffic from a previous appointment and will be a little late. Offer them coffee while they wait and return to your desk to get back to work. There's nothing wrong with *that*, right? You needed to get work done. But, you just left them to sit and wonder: "Is this a common occurrence? Is my business really important to these people?" You were being a "follower." Your boss was running late and you followed right along in that scenario.

A leader will change the scenario to what's best for the company. A leader will make sure the boss has rehearsed his lines and when he forgets his lines, jump in to ad lib for him. A leader will greet clients when the boss is running late from another meeting, take the clients in the conference room and go over their questionnaire and details to stall for time in a friendly and productive. This may take 20 minutes out of your already busy day, but imagine the difference you just made for the company by making sure the client never noticed your boss was late. This is quite different than telling the client that your boss is late and going back to your desk to get back to work. As a leader, you had your boss's back AND his front (behind the scenes by handling the details and out on stage, in front, by taking care of the client.)

attitude and set the tone of the day for everyone. It's also having the courage to step up and direct your boss. Be the one who stops and asks if they need anything else for the day, rather than skipping out before they can slow you down. Be the one who respectfully asks your boss if you can complete the simple task that you find them doing, when they should be doing something much more important (also known as "entrepreneurial stalling.") Be the one who asks your boss for permission to help them focus on their weekly goals and priority lists by checking with them daily on their progress and helping them prepare for the next day. It may all sound overwhelming, but if at the end of the day your boss has gotten to 50 percent more of those things that desperately needed to be done, wouldn't it be worth your time? Imagine if you actually got the information you needed from him to carry through on a task because you took time to download and debrief with them daily, might it be worth the effort? And if you stepped in and became a team leader, so team members come to *you* for direction rather than interrupting your boss, wouldn't it certainly be worth it? You would most likely end up saving time, not to mention frustration.

Leading your boss means there is a mutual interdependence—you depend on your boss first and foremost for setting a direction for the company, then letting go of the control of day-to-day tasks which move the team in that direction by leaving that to you. You also benefit from unlimited coaching from your boss–they are more willing to provide mentorship to you if it's paying off by taking some of the leadership responsibility off them and shifting it onto you. Your boss depends on a leader to be his eyes and ears. He depends on your reliability, hard work, and integrity. You both rely on one another for successes that will satisfy both of you personally and professionally, and ultimately, satisfy your customers.

Your relationship with your boss is *the* most important element in determining your success in your current role and certainly the single greatest element in advancing within the company. The bottom line is that you have to take the position of leading your boss—they *need* it and *expect* it from you.

So how do you make this happen? It really is much easier than you think. Go back to your toolbox (i.e., the Kolbe, Unique Ability, etc.) and truly understand the way your boss is wired. Let go of all the stories you are carrying around: he is controlling, never follows through on anything, doesn't care, etc. *Read your Kolbe* and *read your boss's*. He can't help the way he is wired anymore than you can help the way you are wired. And guess what, your Kolbe traits might be just as annoying to your boss as his are to you! I am sure he respects you for your hard work and abilities, just as you should respect him for his. You each bring something important to the table. If you really want to support an entrepreneur, remember that they don't have many people truly supporting them–they do most of the supporting. They often compound on this further by alienating themselves and getting defensive, losing credibility by not finishing tasks, or simply by talking in a language others don't understand and not letting themselves ask for the help they truly need–leadership. You need to understand and respect your boss for who he is and authentically try to help address his needs, capabilities, and goals. You need to understand his pain points, what keeps him up at 2 a.m. and his personal communication style.

Once you can truly get inside his perspective, you can get behind his needs. This is not only a great launch pad to work together productively but it is also a safety net for you when you feel yourself getting frustrated and spinning your wheels. You can stop, take a deep breath, and get out of your own perspective and into your boss's. This lets you see how to solve the problem, not just be frustrated about it. We aren't saying that you should be your boss's babysitter. We are saying that if you try to understand and then truly respect and support your boss's goals and what they are trying to accomplish within their business, then you suddenly become a key player when you don't get annoyed every time you have to debrief them five times on the same subject. It's not babysitting; it's simply doing what you have to do to accomplish a mutual goal of serving the client.

If your world looks anything like ours, your day goes something like this: on your way to work, steaming cup of coffee, jamming tunes, and brainstorming your goals for the day, excited to hit the ground running and just knock the ball out of the park. Man, I love this feeling. Head to your desk—"Yeah, I'm bad, I'm bad, you know it" running through your head. One hour into your rock star day and your boss "stops" by your office in that graceful way we all know too well,

"Are you busy?"

You try not to spit out your latte at the ridiculousness of the question. I mean, HELLO, doesn't he SEE the work stacked all over your desk??? You reply, "Um, no" and it all goes downhill from there. Your ideal day is shot. Or alternatively, your reply is so wrought with contempt when your boss asks you to do something that "isn't on your agenda" that he becomes afraid to even approach, and begins to avoid you (and eventually you find yourself out of a job). Most of the time, a boss is either running rampant, interrupting his team constantly, or the team is so self-righteous about their own "to-do list" for the day that the boss is basically out to sea alone with no support.

What to do?

The following is a sample "Rules of Engagement" for having each other's backs (and fronts):

1. The Daily Touch Base

Schedule some "huddle" time with your boss at the beginning or the end of the day to check in. Believe it or not just five minutes on the cell phone with him on the way to work to run through the day's calendar and five minutes at the end of the day to download what happened that day makes a HUGE difference. You'll see the value of the daily dish if you have ever fallen victim to a client calling you to ask the status of a project that your boss promised would be completed a week ago, (and you have absolutely no idea what they are talking about). Or you are out of the office for the one lunch you actually *take* this year, and your boss is frantically trying to find you to ask you to print a report he needs for a meeting. He has asked every person on the team where you saved it. Now *he's* frustrated and your team thinks you are an unprepared slacker.

If you had spent five minutes running through the calendar with him this morning asking: "Who do you want in this meeting?" "What do you need printed or prepared for this meeting?" you would have saved a lot of time, frustration, and inefficiency. Then, download at the end of the day by asking "What is the follow-up for this meeting?" "Did you promise the client anything from this meeting?" If you can't arrange morning AND end-of-day chats with your boss, then try for mornings when you can review the previous day's calendar and prepare for the current day. This is worth the five minutes and will help you avoid time-sucking interruptions throughout the day. If, during your chat, you get the bad news that your boss needs two hours of your time today, then you have a few hours to try to rearrange your own workload instead of a five minute notice when he buzzes you to come on over. This isn't a calendared meeting you have to prepare for. It is a five minute "touch base" at the beginning and end of the day.

Remember, to make this tool work, YOU have to manage the discussion or it will become a one-topic conversation or an all-out chat session about nothing important. Have the calendar in front of you and quickly move from appointment to appointment by asking your key questions listed above. I like to talk to my boss on his cell phone while he is driving into work. The conversation can only be as long as his drive (20 minutes or so) and when I hear he has parked his car, I say, "OK. I hear you are in the parking lot. See you when you get inside." Even if he doesn't have a meeting to go right into, there is the receptionist and three other team members who will, no doubt, distract him before he gets to me to keep the conversation going. As a back-up plan I jump on the phone and start returning phone calls so by the time he is at my office door, I am on the phone! This keeps the meeting short and to the point. If we were to meet face-to-face in the office for a morning huddle, then it is much harder to stay on-topic and keep it short. (Now that this is in print and my boss knows my trick, I'll have to find a new one…)

2. Speak the Same Language

Your boss has most likely employed people before he lucked out and found you. This means there is going to be baggage left behind by previous employees, just like you may have baggage from your previous bosses. Your boss has probably been offended, disrespected, and unappreciated by others. Unfortunately, there are some key phrases or actions that you might accidentally stumble into that trigger the unpleasant memories of this baggage left behind. In order to not only work together, but also succeed together, you have to have a common "lingo" that will support each other, stop each other, and move everyone forward. This helps you to avoid stepping into traps and also provides you with "safe" words. This is the best way to keep expectations clean and avoid unpleasant surprises and future blowups.

Check out the chart below to ensure you are speaking the same language as your boss:

What You Said/Did	What the boss wishes he could say and sometimes do	Try this instead:
"Are you busy?"	"No, I'm not busy. I have nothing to do!"	"Are you interruptible?"
"You need to…"	"I don't need to do…"	"Would it be possible for you to…?"
Cross your arms and "check out" the conversation while making a mental grocery list	"I can pay someone else to act like they are listening to me."	"Let me stop for a minute and make sure I understand what you want?"
"You said…"	"Don't tell me what I said."	"What I heard was…"
"What am I supposed to do about that?"	"I'm asking you for help."	"What can I do to support you?"

Start complaining without permission then get upset when he tries to handle the issue for you	"Why are you wasting my time? I have 22 phone calls to return."	"Do you have a minute? I need to get something off my chest. I am not asking you to do anything right now; I just need to say this."

You get the idea. Your boss must be able to view you as a counterpart and be able to trust you to be 100 percent authentic with him at all times. You are the eyes and ears of the business. So, always do what you say you'll do, have integrity with the team and never, ever talk behind your boss's back no matter how tempting it may be.

3. Daily Progress Report

Reporting is the best way to capture in writing what is important, to ensure that you are both on the same page. If you want your boss to value you and your contribution to the business, be sure to report it daily. I have worked with some people who get so offended and frustrated that their boss doesn't appreciate what they do, but they never take the time to report their progress to him. Remember, he doesn't have to time run behind you each day to see what you did.

You may have heard this referred to as: CYA (cover your ass), but I look at it differently. My boss isn't "questioning me" and I am not kissing up. I am simply reporting my progress. CYAing is reactive: just in case something goes wrong, you have covered your backside. Reporting progress is proactive: it is a daily process of letting your boss and your teams know your contribution and your value. I make this a required practice with *all* of my team members. If my boss knows that I landed three new clients yesterday by following up with them and collected two outstanding invoices, do you think he will care if he sees me chatting at the coffeepot the next morning? No! He will probably stop and congratulate me on the good work! However, if he has no idea what I did the day before because he was in meetings all day and he doesn't know I was working hard at my desk, he may get the wrong impression if he sees me chatting at the coffeepot because he has nothing to compare it against.

Daily progress reports also let your boss know that you completed the things he asked you to do. This lets him not only appreciate your work, but also cross it off his mental "to-do" list. He won't have to wake up at 2:00 a.m. wondering if you mailed that important package or scheduled that important meeting.

Finally, these progress reports let your boss (or you if you have your team report to you) keep a finger on all areas of the business. They know at a glance each day if new referrals are coming in, money is collected, projects are moved forward, etc.

You work hard–don't be afraid to report it!

Now, remember, this is your BOSS you are dealing with. This is not a dissertation including how many times you visited the ladies' room. They don't care. Your progress report should not be filled with justification and CYAing. It's a bullet-pointed, succinct, PROGRESS report–what you accomplished, what you moved, and things that impacted the business that day. It's a snapshot that your boss can quickly read and move on. Here are two samples of this daily report, one from marketing and one from a production person.

Sample: Laney's Monday Progress Report:

1. Followed up with Mr. Smith–going forward–$7,000 fee-appointment is scheduled.
2. Scheduled new prospective client appointment for you for next week– referred by Mr. Jackson.
3. Scheduled follow-up meeting with Mr. Jones that you requested–it is two weeks from now.
4. Scheduled workshop for you with Rotary Club in March on business planning. Scheduled time to prepare.
5. Scheduled meeting we discussed for you and marketing team on Friday to go over new brochure.
6. Called to schedule meeting you wanted with Mr. Brown–left message. I will call again tomorrow.
7. Did not review and revise brochure yet for Friday's meeting–is priority #1 tomorrow.
8. Mailed new client package to Mr. Johnson.

This is a report of Laney's PROGRESS. It addresses the significant things that needed to be done. Even if some are not completed yet, the boss hasn't forgotten them and expects them to be completed. This system is much more productive than the boss having to buzz Laney to ask me how she's doing on that brochure and Laney replying, "Um… I plan to work on that tomorrow…."

Sample: Laney's Tuesday Progress Report:

1. Mailed out all annual client invoices–total of $100,000 in invoices.
2. Mailed all letters you dictated today.

3. Made revisions for Brown agreement you requested for your meeting tomorrow–it is in your inbox.

4. Made revisions to Jones agreement–have two questions when you have a moment.

5. Scheduled time for us to work on Jackson project Thursday afternoon–I will get with you to see what should be printed for this.

This progress report not only provides a succinct update on Laney's progress, but it also highlights Laney's value. Look at all the bills she mailed out today! The boss won't wake up at 2:00 a.m., wondering if Laney has the documents ready for his meeting with Mr. Brown tomorrow. He is now aware that she has some questions to finish the Jones agreement. Laney has eliminated the need for her boss to have to ask her or wonder about any of these issues.

See the key is *Be Proactive*–not *Reactive*. Lead, don't wait and follow.

4. Confidence/Communication Builders

To build a professional working rapport with your boss (trust) you need to protect their confidence. Remember, it's not all about them, but really, yeah, it is all about them. They are your star performer in this play. So you need them focused, energized, pumped, and prepared for the show. If all they get between meetings is notification of client complaints, emergencies, team tattle-telling, and budget problems, are they really ready to go in and land a big client? Relationships are like bank accounts–you have to put enough funds in to cover your withdrawals. And look how many people are withdrawing from your boss's account. Try to find some ways to put it back.

Why should you go through the effort to manage your boss? It gets RESULTS. It's not about babysitting; it's about getting results and value creation. It is in our opinion that your #1 job as an intrapreneur is to protect your bosses' confidence. A confidence builder is where your coaching (and growth) starts. You aren't cheerleading; you are leading the direction of the day. You're investing in your boss' emotional energy level for tackling the big plans you have for him that day by redirecting his attention to some positive news to counteract some of the stress and negative news. You are depositing into his bank account, and at the same time, you are increasing his confidence by providing a positive report and by subtly letting him know he can count on you to keep things in order, prepared, and covered.

Confidence/Communication Builders

1. When your boss is out of the office for one or more days, call and leave them a voicemail letting them know what their first day back in the office looks like. There is nothing worse than showing up ready to tackle some projects and having no idea an important client meeting was scheduled for you your first day back. You aren't dressed appropriately or mentally ready.

2. Do not give your boss bad news before they teach a program or walk into an important meeting. It can wait until afterwards! If they can't do anything about it at the moment and the building isn't on fire, don't distract them by giving them something to fret over in their mind while they are in a meeting and are unable to do anything. You also want to protect them from other team members who like to run and blab bad news to them as they are walking onstage.

3. If your boss is overwhelmed find three positive things to tell them that day. For example, if you pass them in the hall, briefly mention that you just received a phone call about a referral. Remember how many times a day someone tells your boss something bad like "bank account is low, client is mad you haven't finished their work, computers broke, need a new server..." Be sure to give them good reports too!

4. Let your boss know the nice things people say about them. This increases their confidence as well. In fact, you can type a compliment up, print it out, and put it in their organizational notebook so they are reminded that they do in fact make a difference for their clients.

5. When you leave for the day, buzz your boss and let them know you are leaving and ask if they need anything else. Discuss with your boss if they are okay with you buzzing into a meeting to do this. Also, be sure check in about 15 minutes before you actually need to leave, in case they do ask you to do something, you aren't running late if you have kids to pick up or any appointment to make. At the end of each day, e-mail your boss what progress you made on things they asked you to do (Your Daily Progress Report). If you don't tell them you did it, they won't know you did and will wake up at 2:00 a.m. worrying about it.

6. Write down your suggestions for helping and discuss how to do it. For example, if you think returning phone calls for your boss and seeing if you can handle the calls will help reduce the amount of time they

spend on the phone in nonproductive activities, discuss it with them and how you propose to do this, i.e., I will ask detailed questions from the client, then get an answer from you and relay it to the client. This avoids lengthy chats for you and the client and actually gets a faster response to the client.

7. Don't make the boss (or anyone) wrong. Be honest and straightforward about what is working and what is not working in the business (not disrespectful, but honest). Remember it's not about right and wrong, so don't make them wrong and don't get defensive. Don't say "YOU have to…. Or YOU didn't do this." Simply ask, what didn't work about last week's phone call buildup? How could we have handled it better? Usually people will 'fess up and be honest about their shortcomings in an effort to improve things. However, most will get defensive if made to feel wrong. Then you get answers like "Well I was busy. I had 10 client meetings, etc." When everyone moves to protect his or her work ethic in question, the problem never gets solved. Keep it about what is working and not working–not about who was right or wrong. Look for possibilities and resolutions–not blame. If your boss NEVER returns all his calls, maybe the current method "doesn't work." It doesn't mean your boss is wrong, or even if you think he is, telling him that isn't going to make him return his calls. He isn't stupid; he understands the importance, but it still doesn't solve the problem. Try a different method. You return calls and patch them through to him at a "phone call time." Schedule mini phone appointments to return calls and look for ideas to solve the problem. Don't keep beating a dead horse and pointing out the problem.

8. Build in time for ideas so you can control them from interrupting production times or meetings that are not "idea" meetings. By allowing time for "idea time," which is a necessary part of growing a business and keeping your boss's enthusiasm intact, you can protect other times from being hijacked into idea time.

9. Delegation by Abandonment: Delegating up is not the same as managing. Managing is not the same as leading. Leading is taking the reins and steering the ship. Your boss may set the course, but you keep the ship on its path and overcome obstacles that come up along the way. You keep your boss informed of the weather so they can adjust the course as needed (i.e., production, finances, marketing, etc.). Leading is also getting others to stay on course with you, or removing them from

the ship if they are leading it astray. One of the insidious things that will undermine leadership, yours and your boss's, is delegation. From the team's end, many will "delegate up." This is when someone hits a roadblock and instead of trying to solve the problem, he or she hands it back to the person from whom he or she received it, usually you or your boss. This is delegating up. Work flow is supposed to go down, not up. Delegating up causes bitterness from your boss and they begin to question why the "delegator-upper" is even there.

The reverse is the leadership team delegating by abdicating responsibility for something. It's handing a project over without giving all the proper tools and running for cover. You probably have received these projects before–the things you have no clear idea what you are supposed to do, what the purpose is, what your budget is, etc. It's the mess that is dropped on you and left. This causes the team to lose trust in their leadership team because they aren't being giving the tools and opportunity to WIN. They are set up for failure. The team can't achieve a goal without knowing what the goal is and what their boundaries (i.e., budget, timeline, etc.) are.

10. Permission to be honest and keep your boss honest: This is a tough one, and you and your boss will certainly step on occasional landmines in this area, but you can't shy away from or overlook this. To truly run a business together you must have permission to be honest and open with your boss and also to hold him accountable for staying honest. We don't mean honest like integrity. If your boss is cheating, stealing, etc., get out now. This kind of honesty is meant to give true opinions and to point out when your boss is either not being honest with himself or not keeping his word, as in not doing what was promised, misjudging a situation or employee, etc. First and foremost, you must have his permission; you literally have to ask for it. If your boss is going off on a tangent about something that just isn't factual, literally stop him and respectfully (not arrogantly) ask if you can "be honest" with him. If they say no, don't argue with him. But don't agree with his untruth either. You will usually surprise him, but he will agree that you can be honest. Then be honest. Don't blame, but be honest. Your boss sometimes remembers things differently than they actually happened, so be honest and tell him that this has happened more than once so that there is something about how their instructions are landing with the team that just isn't working clearly. Redirect the tangent to a conversation about how can we put "rules" in place for communicating

to ensure the message is understood correctly. Now remember, it works both ways so you have to be willing to let your boss be honest with you too. You don't have to agree, nor does he, but you have to be willing to participate in the conversation.

11. 3rd party credibility: There is enough limelight for both of you. Often you can slide into joking about the boss to clients, or team members, but remember these people have to trust your boss and have confidence in him. Be careful what impression you are giving by what you are saying. If people think your boss is a moron, are they really going to hire him? In return, your boss needs to give you credibility as well. If he wants clients to trust you enough to talk to you and not always need him, he has to introduce you as someone he trusts and values, so they will too! This can be as simple as having the team be trained to say "he is unavailable at the moment, but his assistant can certainly help you with that" rather than saying "oh he isn't in yet," and dumping them in voicemail. First of all, people come to their own conclusions and it's never that you had an early breakfast meeting; it's that you slept in late. Voicemail can't create confidence. It's better to have an assistant take a detailed message and schedule a time for you to return the client's call so they know when their problem will be addressed.

12. Propose solutions, not problems: If you want to be respected, help solve problems. I know its cliché, but until you have been on the receiving end of other people's problems, you cannot truly understand how frustrating it is to have someone dump a problem on you. Then when you suggest a solution, the person shoots down every suggestion you have. "No it doesn't work like that, no it takes longer than that, no I already tried that…" Give your boss the tools and information to solve the problem. Clearly state the problem, what you have already tried and didn't work, what's in the way, and your suggestions for moving forward. Include the amount of time, money, and people it will involve.

Example:

Mr. Johnson sent us a letter complaining that we took too long to complete the work on his case. I reviewed his file and drafted a reply letter from you apologizing for his disappointment but also outlining the number of times I requested information from him to complete his project and haven't received any response. He has paid us more than $5,000, and is due another $3,000. I ended the letter by bullet-pointing exactly what we need from him to complete the project and once received, I can have it done within one week. Can you review the letter?

Or:

Mr. Johnson wants a refund on his fee. His deal fell through, so he wants his money back from us. I checked his file and we did do some work, about half of what we anticipated before the project fell through. I suggest we either give him 100% as a credit towards future work with us or refund half in cash. What do you think and I can reply on your behalf?

Or—here is a kicker:

Mr. Johnson is upset that we took so long to complete his case. I tried to explain that I've left multiple messages to schedule his next meeting, but he is irate and insists on talking to you. Is it okay if, rather than waste your time on a phone call, I'll schedule his next meeting while I have his attention and I will sit in the meeting as well to get all the follow-up info so we can complete his work within 2 days of his meeting? I will schedule time on my calendar the day after his meeting to complete the work for your review, and time on your calendar to review it so it doesn't get overlooked. (Even though the boss has to deal with this problem, you didn't delegate up or abandon him. You are taking it on the chin too and helping solve the problem.)

The GUT Check: Do all of these suggestions make sense, but you still feel an internal disconnect or hesitation? The bottom line, folks: you need to take care of yourself. How do you know when a conflict is a personality/personal issue and you just can't work with your boss? How do you know when you simply will not grow personally/professionally here any longer? The age-old litmus test is the "gut" check. Ask yourself the following questions to determine if it's time to move on:

- Do I respect him for his humanity, compassion, and integrity towards others?

- Am I being heard and respected here?

- Have I had this exact conversation multiple times within the past 12 months with this person? Is this a repeated pattern?

- Do I get out of bed every morning dreading going to work because I know I am either going to be demoralized, screamed at, or defeated in everything I touch because my boss cannot get out of his or her own way?

- When I walk out of a meeting/conversation with this person, do I feel like the life has been sucked out of me and I've been beaten with a hammer?

You're not going to like this, but if you only answered yes to one of the above questions and had to stop yourself from getting all heated up and talking out loud like you were telling the ladies the whole dramatic story over Cosmos, it is time to go. Trust us. We have been there. You cannot make a difference and the writing is all over the walls. There are only two kinds of suffering---long term and short term. You choose. Do you want to continue to suffer long term and have this same conversation a year from now? Or do you want to endure short term suffering and do something about it. Consider the possibility that there is something more nurturing, growing, and rewarding waiting for you on the other end. Take responsibility, take immediate action. Don't bury your head in the sand and carry around your suffering stories any longer. It goes back to the first nine items above. You need to have integrity and honesty with your boss: "confront the brutal facts of your current reality and retain the faith that you will prevail in the end."

Now, if you do decide that you are in the right place for you at this time in your life, then start making a difference. Don't follow, lead. You don't learn by simply following others with blinders on, no questions asked. Even if you are entry level and following others for now, learn, take responsibility, set a positive tone, show your value, earn respect and learn to give it. Leading isn't about "being in charge." Plenty of people in charge aren't leaders. Leaders are those who keep people moving down the right path in the direction the business is supposed to go. You may be in the front, directing the path, or you may be at the rear giving progress reports to keep morale up and making sure all the bases are covered. Leaders lead–it's an innate trait. These are simply some tools, techniques, and insights to help you see how leadership shows up big and small in the workplace, and to help you along the way.

Don't be a Yes Chick Action Plan: Schedule check-ins and report daily progress. Download the following knowledge tools from www.yeschick.com; *Tips for Weekly Effectiveness*™, *100% Guaranteed Confidence Protectors*™, and *How to Eliminate Useless Meetings*™.

CHAPTER 7

Empowered Chick

The Key to Empowering
Conversations

*"You gain strength, experience and confidence
by every experience where you really stop to look fear
in the face. You must do the thing you cannot do."*

- Eleanor Roosevelt

Not all of us have had a "tough conversation" with the boss that turned out to be truly empowering, but we have. A conversation where he calls you into the proverbial office to reprimand you and by the end of the conversation you leave so pumped up and raring to turn around whatever you did "wrong."

How is that you say? The answer is that the conversation was empowering. An empowering conversation is the key to having a conversation that produces results, takes the emotional element out of it and eliminates wasting time.

Having an empowering conversation is a skill every leader must acquire. This chapter is designed to teach you HOW to get results from your conversations by empowering others.

What is an Empowering Conversation?

In an empowering conversation, the other person leaves motivated to "OWN IT." You may not be clear on all the nitty, gritty details, but you are never afraid to ask for clarity because you completely buy into the idea at hand. An empowering conversation only has to happen ONCE. The fire is "lit" within and you don't have to keep relighting it. You know the desired result, but not necessarily the path to get there, however; you believe in "IT" enough that you are willing to take action. Yes, it is quite probable that you will fail a few times in the process, but the possible failure is well worth the risk versus. accepting your "IT" to sit on the shelf and do nothing.

We have found over the years that there are 8 Keys to an Empowering Conversation™ that will create a WIN/WIN every single time.

1. **Walk the Walk**

   ...before you talk the talk. The ultimate rule, and subsequently the most ignored, is to make sure you are following your own advice. Bottom line: No one will want to hear ideas and suggestions if you don't have your own bases covered. Practice what you preach. Do you come to meetings late? Unprepared? The first rule to empowering others is to have integrity and follow your own advice.

2. **Honest While Respectful**

   This one can be a tricky line to toe. Make sure you are speaking into dangers and opportunities vs. personal attacks and judgment. Here is one powerful technique you can use to be honest, but respectful.

First, ask for permission to be blunt. Literally, before you say something that you know in your gut might sound offensive or make someone defensive, ask them "May I have your permission to be blunt?" It's not a rhetorical question. At the least, it lets them know to be prepared for something they may not want to hear. It sets the tone for a serious conversation rather than you just blasting them. It's like letting someone know to hold their breath before water splashes in their face. They may still not enjoy the water, but at least they are expecting it. It also shows respect that you are asking them for permission to give them feedback rather than assuming you have the right to critique them.

3. **Facts Without Emotion**

This is really tough to do and we all have to keep it in mind. Emotions are subjective and you don't want to get into a debate over IF something should have stressed you out or made you mad or feel unappreciated. Someone else can't honestly understand how you feel, because he or she may not feel the same way in the same situation. And if I may have YOUR permission to be blunt, let's face it; if you are a woman, anytime you let emotion into the conversation, you immediately lose credibility. Instead of emotion, be prepared with facts. Don't use words like "I feel" or emotion words like "mad, upset, etc." Pack up the tissues for GOOD. Leave the "story" at the door, ditch the judgmental words, and focus on facts and resolutions rather than trying to make someone "understand" your point.

Example: Emotion–"I am so swamped I am stressed out and making so many mistakes."

Facts: "Our average new clients per month have increased from five to eight. This is an additional 15 hours per month of work for me. I find myself rushing to get all the documents done on time and have caught three errors I made. I am concerned that this increased workload, and the time pressure to get it done, is going to continue to cause me to make mistakes."

4. **Don't be a "Yes-er"**

Don't be afraid to say "let me think about it." Too many times we see teams lose credibility with their boss by always trying to have an answer. It's better to be honest and ask for some time to think about something important or to check into the facts than to answer off the cuff, then the next day change your answer. You just look wishy-washy. If you are caught off guard with a question, be honest and say you don't know, and need some time to think about it or look into it. Then follow up and get back to your boss with your thoughts as soon as you have the answer.

5. **Acknowledge**

Along with the tough parts of the conversation you are having, be sure to acknowledge the strengths of a person. You don't just want to point out the wrong things, but motivate them and give them confidence to improve. Sometimes merely saying "I know we aren't seeing eye-to-eye right now, but I want to acknowledge you for hanging in this tough conversation with me" can mean a lot to the other person.

6. **Time and Place**

Pick a time conducive to the conversation you want to have. For example, I actually had a team member schedule a meeting to talk to our boss about a raise directly after his end of year tax meeting with his CPA. You know, the meeting where he finds out the big check he has to write the IRS. It's not the best timing to discuss raises while the boss is still nauseous about his tax bill. Monday morning when your boss has a full day of back-to-back appointments until 7:00 p.m. also may not be the best time to complain about your workload. Choose a time where the boss will be open to your conversation and not distracted by other things.

7. **Don't Pop the Balloon**

The worst conversation faux pas I see a team make is popping their boss's balloon. All bosses have certain things they get excited about such as new ideas, technology… you know that thing they get all perked up over? Time and again I see team members shut their boss down when they are excited. They may be "the voice of reason" but no one likes to have their balloon popped. Don't snap them back to reality with "we have work to do" or "no, we already talked about that" type of comments. You don't have to let the boss run away with a conversation, but be respectful and gentle. After all, if I have your permission to be blunt, sometimes when you approach the boss to discuss things important to you it sounds the same to them, and you wouldn't appreciate it if they shut you down.

8. **Doesn't Work/Works**

If you can adopt this one tool alone, it will make the greatest difference in your communication, production, and growth. Don't blame or make people wrong, things either work or don't work. But don't just let the conversation end there. State and agree what has been discussed and what actions need to happen next to move "doesn't work" into "works." Too many conversations are ideas with no action. People will be more apt to take time to have honest conversations you request when they see they get results.

Blame: "Joe keeps dumping all the new client work on my desk. It's stressing me out; I'm rushing and making mistakes."

Doesn't Work/Works: "It isn't working for me to handle 15 additional hours of client work each month. If I hire a P/T temp, it will free me up to work on revenue-producing activities and I can eliminate the careless mistakes I have been making while rushing. Your thoughts?"

There is no blaming in the second statement. It's stating a fact and a clearly-defined request to make something work that clearly doesn't work.

Don't just list all the things that aren't working. Have some suggestions for things that are. Even if you can't come up with a total solution, put some thought into it. At least have some ideas or narrow down the scope of what needs to be worked on.

The above 8 Keys to an Empowering Conversation™ allows you to be a cause in the matter and in the solution. When having a tough conversation, there are a few simple tips to help you stay on track to an empowering conversation:

- Shut the door. Really, it's that simple. It's hard to be empowering with interruptions and outside distractions.

- If the conversation isn't scheduled, ask if the person is "interruptible." DON'T ask them if they are "busy." We are all busy, but that just puts someone on the defense to start with. Also, it's a sign of respect to ask if someone is interruptible and it lets you see how much that person respects you if he or she is willing to stop to talk with you.

- Turn off cell phones. Nothing is more disrespectful than taking up someone's time for a conversation and then stopping to text or answer your phone.

- Start with a thank you. Again, simple. Start with "thank you for taking time to talk with me."

- Begin with your goal and the "who" and "what." Rather than starting into an explanation that the other person may not follow, start with stating your goal. "I'd like to talk for a minute about how to get better turnaround times. I have some ideas I'd like to share."

- Write down your points. It's easy to get emotional and off track in a tough conversation. Write down your key points to keep yourself on track and avoid getting flustered.

- Begin with the end in mind. Be clear on your intentions. The other person may not agree, but they will respect it. You will get better results if someone respects your position and honesty about it than trying to browbeat them to agree with you.

The Who, the What and the Why

Be clear on what you are taking a stand for: your team, your boss, the company, or yourself. Know the "why," and be clear about it. It's easy to jump into a conversation and it's very tempting to state your opinion so everyone can hear. But don't waste your words. If you are having a tough conversation and you want to leave others feeling empowered, be clear on why you are taking a stand. Whom are you serving and/or helping in this conversation? Why is this important for them? Is it to support them in producing results, for their personal well-being? All are acceptable answers, but you need to know why you are getting into a conversation and whom are you taking a stand for in it. Otherwise you won't know what you are trying to achieve or who is benefiting. Once you know, stay clear in the conversation, the "who" and the "what" you are taking a stand for.

Remember, you have complete permission to take one small step at a time. It takes 30 days to create a habit and eight steps to an empowering conversation. All conversations are created equal and the eight steps can be applied to all. It may sound harder than you think, and it certainly takes practice as the human element will test you every time if they are living in the world of their commitment to be right in every conversation. So focus on the progress you are making, not perfection. You have complete permission to fail forward.

Don't be a Yes Chick Action Plan: Practice the 8 Keys to an Empowering Conversation™ and use them!

CHAPTER 8

Team Chick

Building Your Team and Making it Work

*"If you want to go fast, travel alone,
but if you want to go far, travel together."*

- African Proverb

The team you work with is *the* make or break part of your ability to succeed in the workplace. We've seen exceptional people quit lucrative jobs because of the team players they were forced to work with. We've also seen people take pay cuts and drive an hour to and from the office to work with co-workers who motivate and inspire them. In the workplace there are two sides of the equation, namely, those whom look to you for support, and those whom you look to for support. In other words, are you working in an environment of co-workers who inspire you and allow you to grow?

Where do you fit in? Are you the co-worker who others will drive an hour to work with? This doesn't mean that you have to be friends and socialize with everyone at the office. Nor does it mean that you let yourself become the office psychiatrist who everyone dumps on. (This might make you popular, though exhausted, but it won't inspire an associate to want to work with you because she sees the long-term personal growth and opportunity around you.) It means that you're the person who team members would always pick to be on their side, because they know that you'll get the job done. It means that you're the team member who people come to when they have a work-related problem that they don't know how to solve, because they trust your even-handed decision-making ability. These are signs of a team leader. These are signs of greatness in the making.

I Can Do it Faster Myself

The biggest trap you can fall into is the trap of "I can do it faster myself" and this is one we have fallen into ourselves time after time. The problem is it does take you less time to do something yourself than to train someone new. Of course it does, you already know how to do the task and you are familiar with it. But there are only so many hours in a day, and you can't do everything. If you are overloaded with work and feel you don't have the "time" to stop and train someone how to help you, things will never change. You will continue to be overloaded and overworked. By carving out the time to properly train someone to help you, piece by piece your workload will lighten and ultimately free up your time to focus on your "future" growth activities.

The cardinal rule for "moving on up" is to replace yourself with a highly trained replacement for your current role, this allows you to create a bigger future for yourself. It's critical that you do it properly. This means that in order for training to be effective it needs to be in writing and it needs to be step by step. Casual verbal references to "the way we do things" won't work.

Laney once worked at a law firm where they hired a new attorney so they could turn around work for their business clients faster. They were getting behind and clients were noticing. Just after a month, the "boss" complained that the new attorney took two days to do something that would only take him 15 minutes to get done. While Laney suspected the statement was a bit of an exaggeration, she reminded him that it took three weeks to find an available 15 minute time slot on his calendar to complete the task. The task was completed faster with the new attorney taking two days to do it, because she had the two days available *now*. This is how a team works. Teams can unlock the gridlock or bottleneck of workflow and allow things to get done faster. So just because you are the fastest at something doesn't mean you should be the one doing it, and it certainly doesn't mean it is the best revenue producing activity for you.

If You Want to Go Far, Go Together

The other devastating effect of "I can do it faster myself" is that you not only harm yourself, but you take away an opportunity for growth for your team. A team that grows together stays together. If you have a quality team, but don't provide opportunities for growth they will get lazy, sloppy, or leave. To empower yourself and your team, create growth opportunities for you and them. As you move forward, they move forward in unison.

Systems Save Time and Sanity

One of the best things you can do for yourself and your team is to force yourself to stop and write down step-by-step instructions for anything you have to train a new person or another team member on. We know, we know… it's time consuming and painful enough to show them how to do something, much less write it down step by step. But sometimes that new person doesn't work out, and you end up training another new person and another new person until you find that perfect fit. To save your time, and more importantly your sanity, putting pen to paper and writing down the instructions and placing them in an instruction manual, WILL save you time the next go-round. After writing the instructions, let the person you are training attempt to follow the instructions without you chiming in. This will let you see if you missed any step that needs to be added in. And if after 90 days they still don't work out, at least you have a training manual for the next person that comes along. Look at that! You're already saving time.

Working Within Your Passion

In Chapter 2, we discussed finding your passion in the workplace—isolating the things that fulfill you, and learning how to spend most of your time doing them. A strong team provides you with the structure to spend more time doing the work that you're passionate about. There are other people out there who love to do the things that you hate most. They really do exist.

Laney, for instance, hates anything to do with accounting and, as shocking as it may seem to her, there are people who absolutely *love* to handle the numbers, and receive extreme satisfaction from making sure things add up at the end of the day. (Such people may have a hard time comprehending how people could hate such a task!) Molly, on the other hand, absolutely despises doing sales. She'll wake up physically ill if she has to make a sales call, and will come up with every excuse in the book to avoid doing it "today." Laney is stunned that some people wouldn't leap at the opportunity to teach a seminar. However, a team member once told her that she'd sooner chew off her right arm before she'd get in front of a room of people and speak.

Each of us has their own Unique Ability. The key to creating a dream team is to determine the skills your workplace needs, and then balance your team with people who excel in each of those areas. Let us restate: not just excel at those activities, but *thrive* on them. It's vital to find that special person who'll go the extra mile to perfect the job, because she loves what she does and can't stand to see it done less than perfect.

If there's no balance to your team, there's no platform for your growth. If everyone on your team loves to meet with people and market, who's going to actually get the work done back at the office and deliver on the promises made by the sales team? You'll initially impress people with your group of marketers, but you'll quickly lose business by not being able to get the work out the door. If everyone on your team loves to write, who's going to do the bookkeeping? Your budget will be a mess. Balance is key; it ensures that each person is doing what they love at the same time it helps the team to thrive, ensuring that each position is filled with a passionate team player.

Making Your Dream Team Come True

Your team at work is very similar to a sports team. (Even if you don't like sports, work with us for a minute, because this analogy is quite apt.) Most sports teams have salary caps. They can only pay out a certain maximum amount of money for salaries. If they pay salaries over and above that cap they'll be severely penalized. Your company works in a similar way, not so much with a salary cap, but with a budget. It can only afford to pay a certain amount of money for employee compensation. The trick is to make sure that your team is getting what it really needs for the money that you can spend. If you *must* hire a high-priced new member, make sure that she's worth eating up your budget. Occasionally, you may be able to eliminate two middle-salary people and replace them with this more expensive, fantastic person. The one higher salary will still cost less than the combined salaries of the two you've let go. The opposite could also be true. Instead of a highly-paid upper-level team member, you can hire two more entry-level employees for the same cost and literally get more done. This happens a lot in offices where they don't need more homerun hitters; they just need more singles hitters or better fielders.

Think dream team. Not good team, not okay team, but *dream* team. Look at dream teams throughout history, like the 1992 US men's Olympic basketball team, which included Michael Jordan, Shaquille O'Neal, Magic Johnson, and Larry Bird. Not good players-*great* players.

Think of the NASA team that brought the Apollo 13 home. Not a good team but a great team.

How about the 2004 US Olympics women's softball team? With a balance of outstanding rookies (Jenny Finch, Lovieanne Jung, Natasha Watley, and Cat Ostermann), and incredible veterans (Crystal Bustos and Lisa Fernandez), Dream Team USA absolutely dominated their opponents—outscoring them 51-1 in nine games. *Fifty-one to one!* They had it all—power, hitting, pitching, speed, and defense. Most important, they utilized a team approach.

The worst thing you can have is a good employee. That's because you want *great* employees. Bad employees are easy—they perform poorly, you let them go, and move on. It's the good employee that gets you every time. She may not be doing anything to get fired, but she just isn't doing anything great to fire up the workplace. Good doesn't make history. If you only have so much budgeted to spend on salaries, don't waste your money on good. If you do, you won't be able to afford great when great is available. Even worse, you probably won't even be looking for it.

The Absolute Biggest Hiring Mistake

There are many techniques to hiring, training and developing teams, some of which we cover later in this book. No matter how many people are on your team - if it's just three of you or 50 of you-there is *one key* to hiring that is an absolute and can *never be ignored*. When dealing with people, and team members are people, it's hard to deal in absolutes, but it's absolutely critical. Sometimes people defy the rules or the expectations, but this one is a definite. The key is hiring *100 percent of the time based on integrity*.

Merriam Webster's Definition of Integrity

1. *Firm adherence to a code of especially moral or artistic values:* INCORRUPTIBILITY
2. *An unimpaired condition: SOUNDNESS*
3. *The quality or state of being complete or undivided: COMPLETENESS*

Our Definition of Integrity

Do what you say you're going to do when you say you're going to do it, and be 100 percent authentic every step of the way.

Integrity is one of the most crucial, yet mind-boggling of terms. Integrity is an "airy fairy" term rarely understood. To give you perspective, it is sometimes used with "moral," but in actuality, it is separate and distinct. Let us help clear up the distinction and more so, share why it matters in the hiring process.

If a team member doesn't have integrity, it doesn't matter how talented they are, how good they are at what they do, how many hours they work, or anything else you normally judge performance on. The bottom line is a person without integrity is not a fit for your team. Not only will they eventually fail, but they will poison your team and you will lose *great* team members along with them. Worse yet, team members who don't have integrity will *stay* and continue to be a communicable disease to every client and new team member that walks through your door if you continue to allow their poison to exist and permeate your business.

If your gut is saying "something doesn't feel right in the belly," don't even think of hiring them. Integrity is not trainable. You have it or you don't. You can't pay for it, work harder for it, or teach it. It's either there or it isn't.

Let Molly put this into perspective for you with a real life example...

Amy passed every interview, Kolbe, and reference check with flying colors. Less than five days into the job, red flags were popping up everywhere. Here is one simple illustration-and you won't need much more than this. This is *more* than enough evidence. It started off with her first business trip on the proverbial company dime where her room service bill was $65 for one person and one dinner. Let me paint the picture. She was the single mom of two teenage boys who were getting ready to head off to college with her annual salary was $19,000. This was not a CEO making six figures used to perks like expensive room service. This was a person with the entitlement mentality that she was going to get fat (literally with a $65 meal!) off the company hog. This is lack of integrity. It doesn't need to be more complicated than that.

Keys of Integrity

Integrity is a tricky thing. Sometimes people with the least amount of integrity are knowledgeable and riddled with skills. They also can have the most talent, charm, and charisma. But skills and knowledge aren't enough.

In fact, these should be the last ingredients to look for. Don't be fooled into thinking that you can work around a lack of integrity; hiring a team member who's missing it is the biggest mistake you can make. You can pass on knowledge and your skills to employees; but it's far too late to teach integrity.

Here are some simple ways to identify someone who has integrity in the workplace:
- She does the right thing, even when nobody's watching.
- She takes a complaint directly to someone who can do something about it.
- She abstains from office gossip, even when others are wallowing in it.
- She tries to help co-workers find remedies for their complaints instead of being a co-conspirator in creating a belief that the workplace "sucks."
- Her "weekend" life is totally in line with her "weekday" life.

Here are some signals that a person has no integrity:
- She talks about cheating on a boyfriend.
- She shops 'til she drops, even though she complains that she doesn't make enough money.
- She slams friends, neighbors, and ex-co-workers.
- She starts sentences with, "Don't tell anybody" or "You didn't hear it from me." If it's spoken out loud, expect that it will be repeated.

Team Hires Team

When you're hiring a team member, you should first decide who the best person is to interview a candidate. For the interview process it's important to know what the team needs to be complete. Therefore, it makes sense that the best person to interview and screen potential new employees is…drum roll… the team itself! After all, who works hand in hand with the team the most? Who sees what the team does when the boss is away or in a meeting? Who's most impacted by a team member's poor work or lack of integrity? The rest of the team, of course! Sometimes, the boss is the last person to feel the pain of a bad team member, because everyone else has been covering and picking up the slack and dealing with a bad attitude for a while.

The most successful hires we've seen have all been interviewed by the team and screened down to a few finalists before a final interview with the boss. The team will pick up on a good or bad attitude, know all the ins and outs of a job, and recognize who'll be a good fit for all aspects of the position, not just the side that the boss sees.

The Group Interview

One of the best techniques for hiring is the group interview. Here's how it works.

Invite all your potential candidates to attend a group interview. Let them know that you won't be asking them questions in a group format, but you'll be presenting information about the job, the company, the job's duties, etc. If they're still interested after that experience, applications will be distributed for completion. One-on-one interviews will be scheduled for the following day.

Create a PowerPoint presentation introducing the company, the team members and their roles, and explain the job that you're in the process of hiring for. Include all the responsibilities, and list benefits and pay. Put anything that might be a problem out on the table, such as occasional evening overtime, occasional travel, etc. Remember, a true interview is a two-way street. In addition to making sure that the person is a good fit for the company, make sure that the company is a good fit for the person. Your goal is to eliminate anyone who isn't going to like the place before you spend time and money training her.

Always have a team member in the room greeting and chatting with the candidates. You'll be amazed at what's said. Make sure that your team member has a copy of all resumes and that each person receives a name tag when she arrives. This lets your team member make notes on the candidates' resumes while you're presenting. You can immediately eliminate people who make negative comments or show any red flags.

Molly goes a step further, and has another team member pose as a candidate and sit in the room. At some point, Molly will leave the room, and the "spy" can assess the various candidates' attitudes when there's no supervision. This technique allows you to find and eliminate that person who has no integrity and is the poison apple before they can contaminate your team. If you use the "spy" technique, make certain that your PowerPoint presentation doesn't include her in the visual representation of your team!

The One-Question Interview

There are hundreds of great interview questions that you can ask, but we can narrow them down to one that will tell you exactly what you need to know. It goes like this:

"If you come to work here, and a year from now we're sitting at this table conducting your one-year review, what would have had to have happened for you to be happy and feel fulfilled working here?"

This answer will tell you what a person wants out of a job, what she aspires to, what her goals are, and what she's passionate about. It will also identify if the person has no idea what she wants because she'll have difficulty answering the question. You may not want a team member who has no goals or clarity about her future. You may also discover things that don't mesh with the company. For instance, one candidate told Molly that she hoped to have completed her Master's Degree in computer science, but Molly's company had no need for a computer tech on staff. After some discussion, both the candidate and Molly realized that they weren't a good fit. Even though the candidate was qualified, the company wanted a long-term team member, not someone who'd be looking to change industries in a year. On the other hand, we love to hear people who say that they'd like to look back and see that they had accomplished something with their team. It's also great when people are honest and say that they hope to be making more money. Everyone wants to make more money, and if a team member is growing, she *should* be making more money in a year.

Last Piece of the Puzzle

Once you've identified a strong candidate to join your dream team, and she's passed the group interview and the one question test, you should request that she take the Kolbe. This isn't always a make-or-break test, but it will identify any red flags in her ability to fit the role that she's being hired for. If she's a Quick Start and a Follow Thru, for instance, but the role that she's being hired for is a bookkeeper, it could be a red flag since a bookkeeper has to do a lot of follow-through to get all the books balanced.

The Kolbe is a must before we begin training anyone. It lets us know how to train and interact with someone. If she were a Fact Finder, we'd give her lots of details. If she's a Quick Start, we may give broad parameters and deadlines and let her test things out for herself. About 90 percent of the time when a new team member is having a rough start and she's not happy with us, or we're not happy with her, it's a Kolbe issue. We were giving her too much or too little detail. Things quickly get back on track once they are identified and adjusted.

Still Think You Don't Have Time to Train a New Person?

If you're still overwhelmed by the thought of training a new person, think of how much time you're dedicating to dealing with issues of bad employees. How much time do you spend cleaning up their messes, having corrective conversations with them, or calming down your boss when he's in an uproar? Or, if you don't have a bad team member, you may be too busy to hire help. Think of how much time you spend apologizing to clients for something that you couldn't get done quickly enough, or the time you spend looking for something because it wasn't filed properly, entered into the database, or scanned. If you spend as much time hiring as you do on these problems, you'll find the right person for the job. If you cheat yourself and rush through the hiring process, and grab the first quasi-qualified person who comes your way, you'll be spending more and more time deciding to fire her than you spent hiring her in the first place.

We hope that you now realize the importance of a solid team to your own career and start taking the steps to build a solid team with integrity, passion, and potential.

To learn more about hiring the right person, visit the *Smart Hire Solution*™ at www.yeschick.com, which walks you through finding, interviewing, and hiring the right person in greater detail.

On-the-Job Trading

This exercise is great to do every year or two with your team, even if you aren't hiring. Over time, team members pick up new responsibilities at work just because they happened to be there the day it was needed. (This is very common if you lose a team member and others pick up her job duties.) You'll be surprised how much of each team member's time is being taken

up by tasks at which she doesn't excel. When that's the situation, she often doesn't have time to get to the things that she does exceptionally well. It's fun to see how team members will trade responsibilities, getting rid of the things they don't like for things that they do.

Building a Dream Team

1. Make a list of all the major areas of responsibility in your workplace. Don't focus on who currently does what, or the talents of your current team. List exactly what your workplace needs to function and be successful. Here's what a possible list might look like:
    - Talking to prospective clients when they call
    - Meeting with prospective clients
    - Billing and invoicing
    - Updating the website with new schedules and articles
    - Sending out workshop invitations
    - Entering prospective clients into the database to receive invitations
    - Preparing client documents
    - Teaching marketing workshops
    - Preparing materials for workshops
    - Scheduling appointments
    - Ordering office supplies, etc.

2. Group the things that go naturally together so that you have a more focused job description.
    - Talking to new clients on phone, meeting with clients, teaching workshops—these are all things a "people person" may like to do
    - Preparing workshop material, sending out invitations, updating website—these go well together for someone who likes to handle schedules and is good at meeting deadlines.

3. Have everyone on your team write down the things that they're great

at, and the things that they're terrible out at. Use your "tools," Kolbe, and Unique Ability exercises. Have everyone participate and be honest! We all have things we're not good at—nobody's perfect. List the "non-Unique Ability" things first, and end with the things that they *are* great at. By finishing with their "Unique Ability," the exercise will end on a positive note.

4. Match the best abilities to the job role. If you don't have the right people in place—start cleaning house. There are only two kinds of suffering—long-term and short-term. Only you can decide how long you want to suffer.

This exercise helps define where you lack coverage. You might be missing that great team member who is shy and uncomfortable talking to new clients, but really enjoys entering information into the computer and feels satisfied when she keeps materials prepped in advance, and the website up-to-date.

The next time you have the ability to hire a new team member, you'll know just what you're looking for. It's easy to be seduced by a great potential employee when you're interviewing, but make sure that she's great at the abilities you need. She may be capable, but that doesn't mean she's what your team needs.

Don't be a Yes Chick Action Plan: Review the Laws of Replacing Yourself, build your dream team, and learn the method to hiring the right person. Visit www.yeschick.com for the knowledge tool, the *Smart Hire Solution*™, before you make your next new hire.

CHAPTER 9

Growing Chick

Why Becoming a Leader is so Important

*"Management is doing things right;
leadership is doing the right things."*

- Peter F. Drucker

Nurturing and growing your team is a never-ending process. And if it does end, you're in trouble because it means that your team is no longer growing. That's the beginning of stagnation. Like sitting water, your team doesn't just stop growing and stay in place; they start to rot and eat away at all the standards, training, and culture that you've built. If a team isn't motivated by growth, they'll focus on other things that are negative and unproductive. A team that doesn't have goals becomes wrought with gossip, cattiness, blame, and complaining; hence, your work as a team leader is never done. You can either devote time to leading your team, or spend time reprimanding them. The choice is yours. We don't know about you, but we have very little patience for reprimanding.

Why is it my job to lead the team?

Everyone isn't a leader. If you're reading this book, chances are that you are a leader or well on your way to becoming one. The role is both a blessing and a curse. The curse is that you can't stop being the leader that you are even though there'll be times in your career when you stop leading. Maybe you'll be mentally exhausted, or in an atmosphere that doesn't allow your leadership abilities to flourish; regardless, while you may choose to stop leading others for a period, you can't ever stop being a leader anymore than you can stop being a mom, the glue for your family, or a community advocate.

Don't Curse Your Gift as a Leader

This will show up as:

"Why does everyone come to me, I have enough on my plate?" or

"I'm tired of everyone leaning on me!" or

"Is it me, or is everyone else either an idiot or just doesn't care?" (Boy, have I said those things in the workplace!)

You can't run away from your talents and responsibilities as a leader, even if you try, it won't fix your problem, or make you happier. There have been many times that we've wanted to quit our jobs in order to get an easy and "stress free" one where we could show up, do the work well, and go home. We long for a job where we wouldn't have to solve other people's problems, or take stress home, but, alas, a leopard can't change its spots. You can either embrace the leader who you are, or find yourself constantly feeling unfulfilled.

If you're a true leader, you're a beacon in the night. Even as low man on the totem pole, you will draw people to listen to you, and ask the tough questions; in other words, you'll motivate and lead. Others will be drawn to your innate ability to provide calmness and direction in the storm. If you're really honest with yourself, you probably aren't happy when you're not leading. We're not saying that you have to be a 1-800 help line, or wake up at 2 a.m. stressing over things at work, but when leaders aren't in a position to lead, they're like a flower without sunlight. They'll wilt, their colors will fade, and their vitality that always shone brightly will waste away.

As long as you can't rid yourself of this incessant need to lead, why not simply embrace it? Remember, it's not only a curse, but a blessing, as well. Very few people have the gift to inspire others. You can. Look at the difference you make in other people's lives. For example, take a single mother who you're helping build a career. You aren't just helping *her*, you're making a difference in her children's lives too. Few people can provide calmness and confidence in times of change or uncertainty. *You* can. Remember all the people who you've helped keep the faith and not lose direction. Few people have the ability to truly make a lasting, positive impression on other's lives. *You* do. Your ability to lead is a blessing. It only becomes a curse when you can't balance the dependency of others with your own needs.

Why is Being a Leader so Important?

To be blunt, team members who aren't in a growth-oriented workplace with good leadership won't be around for long. In that environment, a good team of unfulfilled and talented members will move on to other places that provide leadership and growth. The rest of the group will become infected with a potentially infectious spirit of gossip and negativity. You will end up firing those individuals to clean up your office. Look at it from a purely selfish perspective: after all the time you've spent hiring and training, do you really want to start all over? Which do you think would be a better use of time— helping a great team member continually find ways to grow, or starting all over interviewing, hiring, firing, and training every quarter?

The Goldilocks Syndrome—Finding "Just Right!"

As a team leader, you'll always be under a microscope. That being said, don't do anything that you wouldn't want your team to do. Your actions set the standard. If you goof off, they goof off. If you cut corners with client work, you give them permission to cut corners on client work.

What is Growth?

Growth doesn't necessarily mean more money or a promotion. While a great team member should periodically be given raises, or the opportunity to earn more money through bonuses and new responsibilities, you shouldn't be constantly promoting and increasing pay out of guilt. A growth-oriented workplace is a positive environment that provides value and opportunity for someone to grow as a *person*. It provides a chance for someone to learn how to become an intrapreneur, and to enhance professionalism. It provides financial growth by helping someone start an IRA. It also helps a person grow as a mother or spouse by applying the listening and team skills at home.

Merriam Webster's Definition of Growth

1. *A stage in the process of growing: SIZE*
2. *Full growth (a) The process of growing (b) Progressive development: EVOLUTION (c) INCREASE, EXPANSION*

Our Definition of Growth

Use your ears twice as much as your mouth. God gave you two ears, but only one mouth, because you should listen twice as much as you talk. People talk to you because they like you; they work with you because they trust you. Use your ears to hear their needs so that you can use your mouth to get what you want with integrity.

The "Goldilocks Syndrome" is not that clear cut. As a team leader, you need to exhibit a careful balance of showing that you're a hard worker, but not making the work *look* too hard. Laney had a team member named Nancy, who worked during a time when the company was short staffed; so Laney had to take on additional work. It was a pretty crazy time. After a few months, Nancy gave two weeks notice. She said that she was leaving because the only way she could move forward at the firm was to take on part of Laney's job, which appeared to be too stressful. Laney realized at that point that she had made a serious mistake by letting her team see her at her so busy and overworked. They saw too many of the long hours she was working, and the backlog of work that was stressing her out. Her job appeared undesirable—no one wanted to do it! It shocked her because she didn't verbally go around reminding everyone that she was working extra hours and doing the work of three people. But as a leader you're always watched closely. Nancy had decided that Laney's job was too challenging without enough reward and the company lost a great team member.

Laney learned from that mistake. After Nancy left, Laney made sure that the team never saw her sweat! No matter what fire was on her desk, she made sure her smile was always in place, and that she was always cool, calm, and collected. She had always done this with her *clients*, but now she made sure she was "onstage" with her team as well. Months later, much to her dismay, Laney discovered that some people on her new team thought she "had it made," and that in comparison, they got all the "grunt work," while her job was glamorous and a cakewalk. To add insult to injury, this came to light on a day when Laney spent eight hours cleaning out years of backlogged filing and cases from an employee's office. She was dusty, sweaty, and in need of a shower. Real glamorous! Laney had gone from one extreme to the other in her team's perception of her job.

With Nancy, she wasn't careful enough to make sure that the team wasn't intimidated by learning new responsibilities. Then she made it look too easy, and no one appreciated what she did. Just like Goldilocks, she found one bed that was too soft to lie in, and the other too hard! And like Goldilocks, she went looking for the perfect balance. She found it by keeping that cool, calm, and collected attitude, and by always making sure that she shared the good things about her job. If someone felt that it was too challenging to be part of a decision-making team that had to terminate a team member, Laney would agree, but also let them know that in most workplaces you may not have the opportunity to make employment decisions. On a weekly basis, Laney makes sure that her team sees the value she brings by sharing with the team the revenue she brings in, new appointments booked, new clients closed, etc. This way, they see that she's helping the business grow. She also encourages other team members to share their accomplishments each week. If her team knows that she's helping to generate the revenue that helps pay their salaries, they appreciate her and don't question her contribution to the team. She learned that she doesn't have to be running around, stressed out, and overworked for her team to know that she's pulling her weight.

Stimulating Loyalty: Doing the Dirty Work

Laney has also learned that she can earn a lot of loyalty from her team by occasionally getting her hands dirty. Offering to answer the phones for the receptionist who has a sore throat and can barely talk earns a lot of appreciation. Staying late to help another team member finish a project so that they can get home earlier to their family earns a returned favor the next time she needs someone to stay late. You don't have to do this daily or even weekly—it's a balancing act. But paying attention and thanking your team, acknowledging their good work, and occasionally rolling up your sleeves and working side by side, or covering for a team member, earns the type of loyalty that money cannot buy.

Sample "Monday Morning Huddle" Agenda

1. Victories: Everyone briefly shares an accomplishment from the prior week. This is a great forum for you to share with the team the value that *you* contribute (as we discussed earlier). It's also a great way to start your meeting with some positive energy. (There's nothing worse than sitting in a meeting of moping people!) Also, acknowledge any team member for compliments that she received. You can present a $5 Starbucks gift card, or something similar. Always do this in a team meeting so that the acknowledgement is public.

2. Review your list of money coming in. This is a list of clients who owe you money, or are waiting for outstanding work to be completed before they'll pay you. It may also be upcoming events that you'll be paid to speak at—whatever it is that makes your company money. You'll need a list of what's outstanding, so you can see what needs to be done to bring that money in the door. We call this devout tracking system "The Monies Map™." (You can find a sample at the end of this chapter.)

3. Discuss the three top priorities for each team member: the "Top Three Gotta's." These are the top three things you absolutely "gotta" do this week. This lets everyone know what everyone else is up to, and helps the "boss" to refrain from unknowingly interrupting someone who has a deadline looming that week. It also lets the team know *not* to book new appointments for the boss if he has a full calendar that week. Then review each person's top list from the prior week to see what he or she completed. Doing this in a group format helps enforce accountability. No one wants to be the person who shows up without her top three priorities accomplished.

If you manage the meeting and keep everyone focused, this should take no longer than 30 minutes for a group of 10 or less. If the group is larger than 10, we recommend you have department meetings prior to handling items that are not relevant to the entire group. You should then use your team meeting for the other items.

Mondays are "Grounding Days," and that's okay! Give yourself permission for Mondays to be nothing but meetings in the morning, and recovery in the afternoon. Return calls, e-mails, and accomplish all the "little" things that are delegated to you during your Monday meetings. Call it a huge WIN! The result is that you'll be able to hit the ground running Tuesday, which will create a productive, kick-butt week, because there'll be no little things hanging around. It also shows efficiency as you complete all those little things right away.

Team Reviews

Many employers are not great at conducting annual or periodic reviews, especially if a team isn't giving them problems. But these are the people who need some focused time and attention the most. Keep them productive and growing. They *need* feedback on what they're doing right, and what opportunities are available to them in the future with your company. As the team leader, you should make sure to schedule reviews at least annually for everyone, including yourself.

Here's a system for conducting a review. This worksheet should be provided to the team member at least a week in advance to complete prior to the review meeting. You and your boss should also complete your copy of the packet prior to the meeting to make sure that you're on the same page. *Always* have any homework, suggestions, etc., agreed to prior to the meeting.

Team Member Growth Map™

Team Member Name: _____

Date of Conversation: _____ Last Conversation:_____

Attendees: _____
_____

TYPE OF EVALUATION:
___ 90 day Evaluation
___ Annual Evaluation
___ Improvement Needed

To Be Completed by Team Leader or Boss Prior to Review:
Growth achieved since last evaluation (new skills or responsibilities):
_____
_____

Areas that need improvement:
_____
_____

Recommendations for growth or improvement (courses, books, etc.):
_____
_____

Other Comments:
_____
_____

Team Member's Signature: _____

Evaluator's Signature: _____

Follow-up evaluation requested?   YES   NO

Follow-up date: _____/_____/_____

Team Member Growth Map™ (Continued)

To be completed by the Team Member prior to the evaluation meeting:

NAME: _____ DATE: _____

Please rate yourself in each of the following areas with regard to your work performance.

E: Extraordinary. Performance exceed expectations.

C: Competent. Dependable level of performance, meets, but does not exceed standards.

I: Improvement Needed. Performance is below expectations.

Employee Rating/Employer Rating

Attitude: Brings positive energy to the team
E   C   I   E   C   I
Growth: Constantly taking action to grow and learn.
E   C   I   E   C   I
Creativity: Contributes new ideas and suggestions to better the company.
E   C   I   E   C   I
Initiative: Searches out resources and resolutions to problems without supervision.
E   C   I   E   C   I
Knowledge of Job: Knows and has the necessary skills to complete their job.
E   C   I   E   C   I
Productivity: Completes work in an efficient manner and an acceptable volume of work.
E   C   I   E   C   I
Quality: Completes work with minimal errors.
E   C   I   E   C   I
Follow-Through: Completes assignments in a timely manner.
E   C   I   E   C   I
Client Service: Creates an extraordinary experience for clients.
E   C   I   E   C   I
Team Work: Work with and supports other team members.
E   C   I   E   C   I

Team Member Growth Map™ (Continued)

If we were sitting here one year from today, what would have to have happened for you to be happy with your progress?

Identify the top three areas in which you would like to make a difference in over the next year.

For each item, describe how you can make a difference during the year. Indicate what is needed to accomplish that (i.e., training, additional team members needed, etc.).

1._____

2._____

3._____

If you could change one thing about your job, what would it be?

How would you go about changing it?

What can I do to support you with this?

If there were one way that you could think of improving our business, what would it be?

If you could change your team in any way, what would you do?

Where do you need additional training?

Are there any roles/responsibilities that you would be interested in pursuing in the future?

What do you see yourself doing in the business a year from now?

What do you want to accomplish over the next 90 days?

If you want to know the secrets to giving empowering employee reviews that keep your team productive and on an eternal growth track, check out the knowledge tool *The Smart Employee Review System* on our website.

Goals, Goals, Goals—Enough with All the Fluff?

Individual Goals

In the book *What They Don't Teach You at Harvard Business School,* author Mark McCormack talks about a study conducted on students in the 1979 Harvard MBA program. The students were asked, "Have you set clear, written goals for your future and made plans to accomplish them?" Only three percent of the graduates had written goals and plans; 13 percent had goals, but they weren't in writing; and a whopping 84 percent had no specific goals at all. 10 years later, the members of the class were interviewed again, and the findings, while somewhat predictable, were nonetheless astonishing. *The 13 percent of the class who had goals were earning, on average, twice as much as the 84 percent who had no goals at all.* And the three percent who had clear written goals? Well, they were earning, on average, *10 times as much as the other 97 percent put together!* In spite of such proof of success, most people don't have clear, measurable, time-bound goals that they work toward.

Remember, a person who isn't up to something positive can allow negativity to seep in. Setting goals is the best way to keep you focused and away from distractions of the insignificant.

Team Goals

It will come as no surprise that we're major advocates of team goals. Having each team member working on individual, professional goals is a great way to keep them growing and playing on the team. Remember, if a talented co-worker runs out of new opportunities, she'll look elsewhere for fulfillment, and you can't blame her for that! The same holds true if she doesn't have balance in her personal and professional goals.

We start a new team member with goal setting at her 30-day review. This gives her enough time to have figured out the basics. At 30 days, she may start feeling overwhelmed by how much she doesn't know. Setting goals regarding necessary trainings, etc. for the next few months will give her something to focus on, and see that she's making progress.

The annual review is a great place to analyze and update your team's goals. Personally, we love when our team shares their goals with us. We usually find that they each like a certain part of our jobs, and we can start training them and letting them grow into pieces of it. This means that we can then move up, and grow into new opportunities as well. If we can't free up some of our time, we can't grow either! Knowing each others' goals lets us all grow together.

First, when everyone works together on goals, it allows you to use your Unique Ability to get something completed. You have talent on your team. Use it! Second, it allows your team to focus and work together, which avoids a lot of "territorial" issues, such as the marketing department thinking that they're more important than the accounting department, and the accounting department thinking that the marketing department spends too much money on frivolous stuff. Team goals allow everyone to understand the purpose of an overall ambition, and how each person contributes to it. If you set a quarterly revenue goal to meet, for example, the accounting department might appreciate that the "fluffy cocktail hour" that the marketing department is hosting will bring in a flood of new client appointments to follow. They may offer to help prepare a budget, because that's what they're good at. The receptionist may offer to make outgoing confirmation calls in her spare time to help the event succeed. After all, it's not the marketing department's event now; it's a *team* event that benefits everyone.

Incentivize!

Every single time we teach entrepreneurs we're asked the exact same question—"How do I get my team to implement these goals when they're so busy already?" The answer is simple: *Pay* them. It's funny what we find time for when a bonus is attached to its completion. It's usually not conscious. "I don't need to get paid extra to do my job," or "I simply don't have the time." But if you give bonuses to team members on the completion of something, it stands out in the crowd of "to dos" by screaming for their attention. It also lets them know that it's really important. It draws their focus to what you consider most important for them to complete. We recommend:

1. **Quarterly team revenue bonuses**

    Always have a team bonus that focuses on bringing money in the door, which makes sure that the company is profitable. We recommend quarterly bonuses. One month is too short, and one year is too long to run at a high intensity without reaping the rewards.

2. **Project bonuses**

    These are group projects with one or more team member working together to implement or create something. A project can be an event, a new marketing brochure, a new website, a huge clean up in the office, remodeling...*any* project that's important to your business to be completed.

3. **Individual bonuses**

Design this perk around the three most important things that a team member does for the company so the company makes money. Yes, we keep going back to money and we forever will. A company without revenue + operating in the red= you're out of a J-O-B. And the folks you were so enthused to make a difference for (clients) will lose out as well. If you offer great client service, you can meet your clients' needs, and make money at the same time!

Examples:

- For a marketing or sales person, reward the number of appointments booked, new clients closed, or money collected.

- For a behind-the-scenes team member, reward should be based on billings collected, work completed before a deadline, or a cost-cutting project on office supplies.

Individual bonuses should be reviewed annually, and adjusted as a team member masters how to achieve what you're incentivizing. Then, the goals should be adjusted so that the employee can grow and achieve more. For instance, begin with a bonus for the number of appointments scheduled. Then, adjust it after a year to the number of appointments that result in the hiring of the company. Encourage the team member to help close the deal by getting preparatory materials out in time and following up to close it.

*"Don't tell people how to do things, tell them what to do,
and let them surprise you with their results."*

- George S. Patton

A Few Things to Remember

Leading can be challenging. Learn to balance the needs of yourself with the needs of others. We'll talk more about meeting your own needs later, but for now, remember that the stronger the team that you build, the more they can support you, and provide you with the opportunity to grow in your career. If you let yourself be surrounded with mediocre support, you're boxing yourself into a corner where you can't get out, because you have no one there to help you. Use the tools and insights in this chapter to create a team that grows and wins together.

Sample "Monies Map"

Client Name	Type of Work	Amount Owed	Expected Date of Collections	Next Specific Action, by who and by when

Don't be a Yes Chick Action Plan: Lead your team, give your team reviews, identify team goals, and incentivize. These knowledge tools available at www.yeschick.com can support you in leading your team *The Smart Employee Review System* ™, and *Incentive Based Programs: Creating a Bonus System that Produces Results* ™.

CHAPTER 10

Tough Chick

The Difference Between
Managing and Leading

"Michael, if you can't pass, you can't play."

- Coach Dean Smith to Michael Jordan
in his freshman year of college

Wikipedia Definition of Team

Comprises a group of people or animals linked in a common purpose. Teams are especially appropriate for conducting tasks that are high in complexity and have many interdependent subtasks

Our Definition of Team

"Family-like" folk who you will stop what you are doing and help, even when it means working late to finish your own tasks. The people you trust to ask for help when you need it and you are willing to invest your time and emotional energy into, knowing together, you can move to a higher level.

Deciding to fire a team member is never an easy decision. Our conscious always has a way of slipping into this decision, and so it should. Firing a team member is a serious decision that impacts not only that person, but their team/family, and should be carefully considered. However, firing a team member also impacts the rest of your team and it impacts you too! It takes a courageous and compassionate person to fire someone with dignity and honesty. We'll talk later in this chapter about how to fire someone, but for now it's important to realize how you handle a termination will define the standard and make a deep impression on the rest of the team.

Even more profound, is the impact on you and your team when you *don't* fire that person that really needs to be fired. When a team member begins to have a negative impact on the rest of the team, you not only lose the "problem" team member's production, but the entire team can get sucked into the black hole of negativity. In space, a black hole literally sucks the space around it into its deep, dark nothingness. So does a bad apple team player. A negative team member will suck other team members into their negative disposition and despair. Everyone's attitude and production will suffer. When making this very important decision, consider not only the team member in question, but consider the cost to the rest of your team and yourself. Do they deserve to work in a negative environment daily? Do they deserve to have their confidence and energy taken by another team member? Do you? If you are in a position where you have influence over other team member's jobs, you have a responsibility to your team to protect them from negative team members. You have a responsibility to provide your team with a positive place to work with opportunities to grow.

To Fire, or Not to Fire, That is the Question

This quote can be no truer than when applied to employees. The enemy of a great employee is a good employee. A good employee is one whom comes in and does their job, enough to get by. They are competent, but not great. They do just enough, no more. They do exactly what is asked of them, but put no heart, no mind into the job. They work for the paycheck, not for the possibility of anything more. And that just-good-enough employee is taking up the space on your team where you could have a great employee who does more than what they are asked, puts their heart and mind into their work, and doesn't just do their job, but helps find ways to grow.

The second type of the "good enough" employee is the employee that has some problem areas, but is fantastic in other areas. It's the person who drives you crazy, but is so good at something that you keep them around.

This chapter will provide you a methodology to evaluating when you should fire an employee and when you should keep them.

Again, there are two kinds of suffering: *long term* and *short term*. The only difference between the two is what you choose on a daily basis.

That Mystery "IT" Factor

So often we work with team members that either have "IT" or they don't. We have good enough team members that are missing that special something that makes them great, but we just can't describe it. What is that mystery "IT" factor that is essential to a dream team employee?

For years we have tried to explain it to others. It's that spark. It's that employee who has a good head on their shoulders; they are motivated with unwavering determination; they are a team player. The tune you can find them humming walking down the proverbial hall is "If I can make it there, I'll make it anywhere." Over the years, some fairly basic characteristics were added. They have a brain; they "show up," i.e., present and alert, not in a fog all day. But still, you can't quite define it. Then it came--that mystery "IT" factor that is a "must" in any dream team employee:

They come with *The 5 Individual Elements*

- Individual motivation

- Individual passion

- Individual determination to learn and grow

- Individual accountability

- Individual integrity

In other words, *"batteries included."*

Managing Versus Leading

Previously, we talked about how as a leader you naturally fall into this role wherever you go. However, it's a slippery slope to be an individual whom provides leadership and direction and one who takes on motivating other people and enrolling them into a greater life day in and day out. It's the key difference between managing versus leading.

You might be in a management role, which means you have specific job duties and results to achieve. However, you don't ever want to find yourself "managing" employees if you are working for an entrepreneur. Entrepreneurs are in the business of change that is an absolute. Until you can truly understand and embrace that, you will find yourself feeling like you are "on the hamster wheel" every day; Groundhog Day again? *Daily* operation consists of "think and act *outside* the box." People need to manage themselves. You can hold them accountable to the results they are supposed to achieve, but the team needs to come with "batteries included."

It is one thing to train a team member, help them solve a problem, or give them advice. It's totally separate and not advisable to convince them to want to be on your team. Trying to motivate, encourage learning and find ways to grow while trying to make a moody or negative team member happy and to see the positive will simply waste your time and emotional energy.

Running around managing and motivating your team allows you to become their emotional crutch. They will lean on you for inspiration, and when you can't provide it, they will quit and leave. And when they leave, they leave you with a team of others who you may have neglected and who now see they get more attention and allowance with negative and non-productive energy. You can reinforce a bad example.

If you are providing a positive work environment with opportunity for the team to learn and grow, you won't have to motivate and convince them to work with you, at least not if they come "batteries included." The work environment and the opportunity in front of them is self-fulfilling and self-motivating. It's your job to provide leadership (what direction should they be working towards, a common goal).

Key Questions

If you are unsure if you are managing or leading, ask yourself these questions:

- Do people come to you to complain so you can provide the pep talk, pat them on the back, and send them back to work?
- Do people come to you with a problem and a proposed solution?

Pep talks only work for so long. Presenting a problem *with* a proposed solution rids you, and your team, of its negative impact and the reoccurrence of hand holding, and creates and nourishes the company's next leaders.

Previously, we discussed how to think of your team like building a Dream Team, with only so much salary available to draft your dream team players. Remembering when evaluating an employee for termination, you only have so much time and money to spend on team members. Use it wisely; use it for "great," not good. And remember as long as you are employing that "good enough" employee, you might be missing the chance to hire that "great" one!

The Smart Fire™ 7 Step Test for Termination

If, after reading this chapter, you have found that you might have a "good enough" employee on your team, or even worse, a "black hole," use *The 7 Step Test for Termination*™ to evaluate whether its time to fire.

Test 1: *Has this employee gone "out of bounds"?*

Every workplace should have a list of "out of bounds" that is shared with the team. This is a list of things that will absolutely get you fired. First, the list makes it crystal clear what behaviors are non-negotiable. Second, it actually allows your team to take chances to grow and step out of their role by knowing they won't be fired for making a "mistake." It separates "mistakes" from "out of bounds." For example, it is out of bounds to curse at a client. However, if your business implements a new "payment required" policy that says clients must be current on payments before they order any new services and a team member informs a delinquent client that they must get current before ordering something new and offers to e-mail them a copy of their outstanding invoice, only to find out this is a very important client who has special payment privileges and they get offended, this team member made a "mistake." They tried to step up and handle a situation following a company procedure, rather than dumping the issue on your desk, and they made a misstep. This is something they would not get fired over. It is an opportunity to stop, educate, and create an "Influential" client system. "Out of bounds" encourages team members to try to handle problems and grow by letting them know what constitutes "you're fired" à la "the Donald" and what is okay to step out and try.

The 5 Smart Fire™ "Out of Bounds"

1. Stealing from the company, clients, or other team members
2. Simple misconduct, or cursing at clients or other employees
3. Creating and contributing to infectious gossip
4. Not taking a problem/complaint to someone who can do something about it
5. Soliciting clients for non-work related business

If a team member is out of bounds DO NOT proceed to the next tests. Fire them. Trust us; there has never, ever been an instance where a "warning" has EVER worked. Let the team know why, so they know you are serious about your "out of bounds." Visit www.yeschick.com for a FREE Exit Strategy Checklist.

Test 2: *Do they exhibit the core values of your business?*

Together, every team should create a list of the core values important to your team. This then becomes the criteria for your team, created by your team. It's the list of characteristics they feel is important to provide that positive workplace.

If you cannot honestly say your team member is exhibiting each one of your core values, then you do not need to proceed to the next tests. They have to go. All it takes is one team member violating the core values to destroy the entire team.

Test 3: *Do you spend more time fixing their problems, than doing your own work?*

A tipping point is always when you realize you are spending more time fixing an employee's problem, or the problems they are causing with other team members, than you are doing your own work. *STOP!* Do not proceed, FIRE NOW.

We know all about the hours and hours spent over a three week period discussing whether to let a team member go. Not a day passed that we didn't discuss (suffer) it. We knew she wasn't a "great" employee, but we were worried about the work we would have to take on if we let her go. Even if we rehired her position, we would have to find time to train the new person. Well, after three weeks we realized the hours we spent discussing letting her go, along with the time we spent trying to fix and motivate her, would have been SAVED if we let her go and never had to talk about it again!

Test 4: *Do you dread seeing them every day?*

Seriously, be honest with yourself. Do you dread seeing this person every day? Do you know they are going to whine about something? Or complain? Or somehow deflate your motivation? Do you find yourself making a quick turn-about when you see them at the end of the hallway? Do you go hungry until they are out of the kitchen because you rather starve than go get your lunch and have to talk to them? Don't feel bad about it. You are dreading them for a reason. Your instinct is telling you something.

Do we even need to say it? FIRE NOW.

Test 5: *Do you not see any improvement in their performance?*

A great team member is always improving. They are learning new things, or better, more efficient ways of doing old things. They are doing things faster, better, and more accurately. If you see no improvement in their performance, it's time for the team member to go. Particularly if you have taken time to retrain them, or discuss your problems with them, which if you are considering terminating them you probably have.

A team member who is not improving cannot stay. FIRE NOW.

Test 6: *Are they coachable?*

This is the easiest test in evaluation. Does your employee take the coaching you are giving them to improve their performance and life? You will be surprised at how many times an employee's job is on the line, and when you give them suggestions, advice, or blatant requirements to keep their job, they ignore you. They have multiple excuses for why things haven't improved, but when it comes down to it, they resisted your coaching. This actually makes things very easy for you. You have taken time to try to help the employee find a way to save their job, but you didn't receive the respect of your time and couldn't try on what was suggested. Fire now and do not feel bad. They didn't even take the opportunity to not only save their own job, but quite possibly create a bigger future for themselves. You can't care more about someone's future than they do.

Test 7: *Do they want to be there?*

The seventh and final test is a deal killer for me. Does this person want to be there? Do they show up like they want to be there, or do they drag themselves in, moping and moody? If they don't want to be there, it's not your job to convince them to be. And I promise you, there is someone else who will want to be there, and appreciate the opportunity.

If they don't want to be there, FIRE NOW.

You can fire while still saving your sanity by following our *Smart Fire Solution*™ knowledge tool found on our wesbsite.

Firing for Results

Firing someone is a powerful thing. Not only do you impact the person you terminate, but you have the chance to let this firing impact your team in a negative or a positive way. The absolute worst thing you can do is to not address the matter with your team and let them make up their own story about what happened. This breeds fear and resentment, and an us-against-them mentality.

When you fire someone you have the awesome opportunity to reset your team. Quite often, while you are deciding to let someone go, some of your team will gravitate to that negativity. It's that black-hole effect. People who never even liked this person will all of a sudden be in their office chatting and going to Starbucks with them. Negativity breeds and spreads quickly. That is why it's so important to remove negative team members before they corrupt the team. When you fire the negative person, be frank with your team about why you fired them. Don't share gossip or confidential information, don't share in a manner that is "talking about them," but let your team know in no uncertain terms that negativity is harmful and you removed that person because you are committed to providing a positive workplace for them, and yourself. If you deliver the message in a gossipy manner, the team will side with them and against you. If you lie and aren't honest about why you fired them, the team will perceive that their actions were acceptable and will imitate their behavior. If you are positive about how things will now be better, you can set the tone for a better workplace and your team will follow.

At the end of the day, we all know long before we fired that last person that they had to go. Does the following ring true—"what did she do all day? "WOW, now that she is gone I realize how many things fell through the cracks," "why didn't we do that a YEAR ago?" The writing's on the wall; if it is bankrupting you emotionally, financially, and from a time perspective, follow the rule of thumb and do a gut check. It is always the truest test.

Firing Checklist

Make sure you shut the door when they leave…

It's important when you fire someone to be organized. You want a clean break to move on from. Don't let this person you fired take up any more of your time or mental energy. And don't leave them a back door to damage your company. Use the check list below to make sure all details are handled when someone is terminated.

Team Member Exit Checklist
1. Formal written response — YES or NO
2. Exact written notice, last day — YES or NO
3. Notify bookkeeping re: final paycheck, benefits, etc. — YES or NO
4. Severance pay — YES or NO
5. Verbal exit interview — YES or NO
6. Letter of recommendation (if applicable) — YES or NO
7. Phone script for future employers — YES or NO
8. Dates employed and eligible for rehire — YES or NO
9. Technology to edit security settings — YES or NO
10. Auto forward on email and change phone message — YES or NO
11. Close credit cards or other accounts (if applicable) — YES or NO
12. Obtain office key, equipment and supplies (computers, scanners, phone, printers, etc.) — YES or NO
13. Phone script for team as to why team member is no longer employed — YES or NO
14. Reminder to store items on server, not C-drive — YES or NO
15. Can we contact them in the future if we have questions? — YES or NO
16. Gave employee last check — YES or NO
17. Personally exit out of the building — YES or NO

• **Don't be a Yes Chick Action Plan:** Identify your "good not great" team members, put them through the 7 Step Test for Termination, fire when needed. Visit the knowledge tools online at www.yeschick.com and save your sanity with the *Smart Fire Solution*™.

CHAPTER 11

Future Chick

Becoming a True Intrapraneur

"Some people go through life trying to find out what the world holds for them only to find out too late that it's what they bring to the world that really counts."

- Anne of Green Gables

Hopefully this book has given you insights, strategies, and techniques to empower yourself as an intrapreneur in an entrepreneur's world. Here's one last concept we'd like to share with you: Beware of emotional vampires by building safety nets around yourself and your team.

Emotional vampires are those people, or sometimes even situations, that constantly drain your emotional energy. They take support, energy, and focus from you, and they can show up in a variety of ways.

Some are obvious. They are the negative, pessimistic types that pull you down, dashing your dreams and goals. Others are more subtle, but just as damaging. They may be the "dramatic" type. Being a dramatic person isn't a good or bad thing–it's just a description. However, drama can be irresponsibly allowed to steal other people's emotional energy. Emotional vampires of the dramatic variety tend to operate in a constant state of emergency and chaos and suck you into this whirlwind with them.

In the office, this might show up as:

- A team member who is always having a personal crisis and discussing it at work
- A team member who is very volatile–possibly argumentative or overly emotional
- A team member who always has a lot of excuses, shows a lack of accountability, or fails to take ownership of their job and/or life

The best way to identify an emotional vampire is to notice when the person consistently takes more than they give. And it's a repeating cycle. Everyone goes through a time every once in a while and needs to pull from a relationship, but this is different. An emotional vampire is more so a way of being, not a situational state. Regardless of their current situation, this person always moves into the vampire role. Be objective about your relationships. Even if a person is really nice, funny, or whatnot, if in your gut you dread interacting with them, but "feel bad" and stay in this unhealthy relationship, the emotional vampire has gotten ahold of you.

An emotional vampire can steal your focus, energy, and confidence. You can waste a tremendous amount of time devoting your energies to supporting an unhealthy relationship versus using those efforts to powerfully move forward in your life and career. Sadly, your efforts will not change or help the emotional vampire. They are not looking to have their problem solved. They are stuck in the role they are in and you are enabling it. If you are serious about helping this person, the best thing you can do is to be honest, while respectful, about their impact on others.

Building Safety Nets

Emotional vampires will drift in and out of your lives. And we all run the risk of falling into certain habits and becoming emotional vampires ourselves. The best thing we can do is to put safety nets in place. These safety nets will protect you in dangerous times and help you achieve maximum results during any time.

Build Your Community

Heed the warning; don't go swimming alone. A buddy coach can be a simple but powerful way to avoid swimming alone in the work place. A buddy coach is someone with whom you can "check in" on a regular basis and share your goals, frustrations, and successes. You should have a scheduled, pre-agreed to time to talk no more than once a week and no less than every other week. A buddy coach call doesn't have to be a long call of chitchat and complaining. It's an intentional call where you share your successes, check in on the progress you've made on your goals, and ask for feedback on your suggestions.

A scheduled buddy coach call holds you accountable. Knowing you are going to check in with someone tends to push us to complete goals because no one likes to show up anywhere and look like the haven't completed what they said they would. It can also prompt us to address and handle frustrating situations because we don't want to keep showing up on a call complaining about the same thing and doing nothing about it.

A buddy coach can also provide you objectivity, perspective, and ideas. It can be helpful to have a buddy coach who doesn't work in your office. If she is in the same industry, that's great. Not being in the same office gives her even more perspective and objectivity. If you do buddy with someone in your office, be careful not to "agree" with each other's opinions and fail to "push back" and hold each other accountable. It can be easy for two people in the same office to succumb to a problem or negativity, whereas someone an arm's length away will keep her objectivity and not feel the emotional impact of the same stimuli that you feel.

Goals – with Definitions and Action Steps

Setting goals also helps us not fall victim to emotional vampires. When you have your eyes set on something bigger, you are less likely to tolerate being held back. The key is to specifically define your goal and create achievable action steps to tackle.

Example:

A non-defined goal: create new website

Defined goal with action steps: Create a new website containing a description of each service area the firm offers and contact information.

1. Choose layout design and colors by June 1.
2. Write all content and submit for proofing by June 30.
3. Collect any downloadable information the website will contain by July 10.
4. Forward proofed content and downloadable content to webmaster by July 15.
5. Complete website draft by July 30.
6. Review draft and provide any revisions to webmaster by August 10.
7. All revisions made, reviewed, and website live by August 30–complete!

See how the second version is specific? Creating a new website can mean different things to different people. Some might think it means having the content created while others expected the site to be up, proofed, and live.

The action steps break the goal into "next actions" that are doable, rather than a big, overwhelming goal. If you are faced with the opportunity to sit and hear an emotional vampire go on about their current crisis or use that hour to complete your next action step, you will be more likely to work on your goal because you can see the progress you have made and know exactly what to do next.

Coaching Environment

Being coached professionally is about being in a future-based conversation. It doesn't mean every idea or concept works for you, but it does mean that you are in an environment and conversation where you and the people with you are looking for ways to have a better quality of life, personally and professionally, while achieving the results they desire. Being in this environment can keep you empowered and help protect you from slipping into habits like gossiping, yes-ing, and avoiding goal setting. Being "up to something bigger" keeps you in a conscious state of focus, movement, and growth.

Feed Your Mind Positivity

We cannot say enough about the power of feeding your mind positivity. Surround yourself with pictures, quotes, and reminders of things that are positive and feed your passion. Literally surround yourself with them. Hang them on a cork board, frame them, and read them daily.

Make a habit of starting each day with something positive. YouTube speeches or performances you find inspiring or moving. Some of my favorites are Bono's speech at the NAACP Image Awards, Coach Jimmy V's acceptance speech of the Arthur Ashe Courage and Humanitarian Award at the ESPYs, and Paul Potts's performance on UK version of American Idol. After taking three minutes to watch one of these, any frustrations or problems I have seem smaller and conquerable.

Feed your mind with books that teach or inspire you. Don't underestimate the power of your brain. The other day I was devastated and my confidence was shot by a tough decision I had to make. Stuck on a plane, I began to read a book that had absolutely nothing to do with the cause of my despair, but a simple statement gave me startling clarity and completion. Simply feed your mind. It will find and interpret what it needs so you can find resolutions, completion, and power.

Drive Tip

If you have a commute to work use this time to listen to audio versions of books that feed your mind. You will absolutely arrive to work more focused and ready to take on your day, vs. arriving feeling out of control and at the mercy of everyone else's needs.

Set Boundaries

An effective way to protect yourself from emotional vampires is to set boundaries. If a relationship is starting to negatively impact you, set a boundary to contain it.

You can set a time boundary of the maximum amount of time you will allow this relationship to have. Or you can set a boundary of what you will discuss or permit from this person. Perhaps you won't permit them to gossip or talk about others.

Be Honest While Respectful

Allowing someone to be an emotional vampire certainly doesn't serve you, but it also doesn't serve him or her. Perhaps they have slipped into habits and aren't realizing their impact on others. Use our *Keys to an Empowering Conversation*™ to be honest, while respectful with this person about the damage they are causing. It is far more empowering to give them the opportunity to realize their status and change it, than to tolerate their undesirable behavior.

Measure Results

In relationships, it can be hard to "cut off" an emotional vampire or refuse to participate in their negative habits. We often allow our guilt to force us to continue in these relationships. We talk ourselves into thinking there is no harm and that perhaps we are overreacting. Measuring results allows you to accurately judge the value of a relationship.

In the workplace, measure the performance of a team member. How much revenue do they generate? How much production do they get done weekly? See if they are actually producing satisfactory results. Often emotional vampires are too caught up in their own turmoil to be effective. Even a mega-producer cannot be tolerated if he is an emotional vampire and pulls down the rest of the team.

Keep Moving Forward

We all have bad days, moments, assignments, co-workers and even bosses that can make our lives miserable. The key is to step into awareness about what is actually happening for us. At that moment we are able to move into an empowered place, take control of the situation, and make a change for the better. When you are having a difficult time, recognize if it's a sign of your depleting passion, entitlement thinking, babysitting your boss, or that you are simply being a Yes Chick. Once you know what the problem is, you can uncover how you can adjust it. Working in this way will leave you empowered to take the steps to get what you want, keep your sanity in tack, and hang on to your spirit in the process.

Use this book as a tool and guidebook for improving both your life and career. Read it again thoroughly and implement each piece step by step, create an intention to make small changes everyday. With just a little attention, you'll notice that things will continue to improve. If you find yourself getting stuck, or having trouble dealing with an emotional vampire or an over-demanding boss, remember, support is always available. Awareness is simply the first step in moving forward. When you recognize that things are going amiss, reach out to receive the necessary support – whether through an accountability partner, coach, or confidant.

Never stop growing. The key to your future depends on your ability to take a stand for yourself and never accept anything less than the best. After all, who wants to live their life as a Yes Chick.

Don't be a Yes Chick Action Plan: Create your future, build safety nets and community, define your goals, measure results, keep moving forward, and above all *Don't be a Yes Chick!*

ACKNOWLEDGMENTS

We would like to acknowledge the attorneys we've had the honor to work with for trusting us to support them in building a powerful team. In particular, we would like to thank our mentor, Steve Riley, for allowing us the opportunity and space to grow, experiment, fail forward and find our confidence and passion. We acknowledge you for seeing us as the powerful, creative women we could be. We would also like to thank Dave Zumpano for the passion, excitement and commitment you bring to our industry daily. We acknowledge you for your belief in us and the value we create. We would also like to acknowledge Rick Randall, Landmark Education, Strategic Coach Kolbe and Atticus for the powerful education you provide that has served as a foundation for us.

Last, but not least, we would like to thank all of the assistants who have allowed us to support you in your professional and personal journeys. We acknowledge your courage to step out of the "Yes Chick" role and create an empowering future.

- *Laney Lyons* and *Molly Hall*

ABOUT THE AUTHORS

Molly Hall

How many of you are sitting in the exact position I was, on the hamster wheel, making "good enough" money and no idea of where you would be in 13 years? Let me save you 13 years and provide you with the direct access to creating a life you want by design vs. default.

If someone would have told me 13 years ago that I would be sitting where I am today, I would never have believed it. See, I began serving in the Entrepreneurial World as "just" and administrative assistant, and I proudly still work there today. I started out by getting a "job" at The National Network of Estate Planning Attorneys nowhere near understanding I was on the path to unleashing my true potential and creating a lifetime profession. I have worked closely with Presidents and founders of national organizations, master level marketers, entrepreneurs and coaches. I can't help but practice the "coach" way of doing things on a daily basis in my work and my life. Without the training I have been privileged to receive I would not be the person, professional, mother or friend that I am today.

Through my years and relationships, I was led to my personal mentor, entrepreneur, CPA and attorney, David J. Zumpano. I was Dave's personal coach for 5+ years and when Dave's national attorney training organization, MPS, LLC, began to grow he invited me to lead his team and I continue to do so today. In 2007 I stepped right into the role of CEO/Director of Member Services/Strategic Planner and Coach, everyday wearing each of these hats. I lead a thriving national attorney training organization in succession with my cutting edge Company dedicated to creating, training and supporting intrapreneur's in an entrepreneur's world. I manage budgets, create marketing campaigns, and develop strategic alliance and all the other "stuff" it takes to run a successful business on a daily basis. In 2010, I was honored to be a contributing author of *Speaking Your Truth: Courageous Stories from Inspiring Women* that hit #3 on Amzon.com. But my true passion lies in coaching and that is evident with the 300+ law firms I have coached over the years. I love what I do and I am committed to making a difference; all while being fortunate enough to work from my home in Parker, CO where I live with my husband Shaun and our spirited children, Aidan Patrick and Ella Ryan.

ABOUT THE AUTHORS

Laney Lyons

I worked 12 years in an estate and business planning law firm for a very entrepreneurial attorney.

I landed there 12 years ago, after a brief stint in the Army. I had just turned 21, been released from boot camp with a knee injury and was temping through a staffing service. I landed the temporary receptionist position at the law firm after I was able to remember the 8 other employees names by lunch time… which doesn't say much for whoever I was replacing! I had completed high school and had a few semesters of college, but no degree and no real office experience. I was definitely 21, i.e. didn't know what "dress code" meant and needed a refresher course on my grammar. But I stuck. I had that "get it done" quality and lucky for me, my entrepreneur recognized a diamond in the rough! Or maybe a bird with a broken wing…but anyways I digress. I had that same quality you look for in your staff – that "bring in on" I can do it attitude.

Now, 12 years later, I have helped create business models and help license them to other law firms. I train attorneys and their team across the country. I've co-led a national Key Assistant Program teaching many of the techniques we will share with you. I've co-authored a book published nationally by Simon & Schuster. I've learned to hire, fire and manage my team, as well as my entrepreneur and I've started a successful business of my own. But that's just what I've done. What I've become is more astounding to me. I went from someone who left college, had no real aim in life, felt embarrassed about her lack of progress and was pretty mad at myself because I knew I was smart, yet was on a path to nowhere special. Those close to me didn't really see it. After all, I was always a smart girl and was only 21, but I knew on the inside of me that this aimlessness wasn't for me. I needed a place to make a difference. I needed a game to play – a game to win. And I needed a team of people I respected to play the game with me. I am lucky to have found it. But luck has nothing to do with 11 years later, having learned the ability to create it, manage it and win at any game I choose to play. I have the privilege of making a difference for key assistants I train and being a role model to young women in my family.

In 2009, I was struck by the struggles of many attorneys I know to keep their firms alive during the economic downturn. I created Your Outsource Resource, LLC to serve as an outsource solution to attorneys who need estate planning drafting and funding services.

Personally, a few weeks after launching the company, I journeyed to Cambodia on a volunteer trip. I fell in love with this country and its sweet, hard working children and have already returned once to the orphanage to teach and continually remind these children how special they are.

DISCARD

CPSIA information can be obtained
at www.ICGtesting.com
Printed in the USA
LVHW011404160621
690387LV00011B/306